D0357332

Unclutter Your Life

Transforming

Your Physical,

Mental, and

Emotional Space

Unclutter Your Life

Transforming

Your Physical,

Mental, and

Emotional Space

By

Katherine Gibson

BEYOND
WORDS
Publishing
I N C

Beyond Words Publishing, Inc.
20827 N.W. Cornell Road, Suite 500
Hillsboro, Oregon 97124-9808
503-531-8700

Copyright © 2004 by Katherine Gibson

All rights reserved. No part of this book may be reproduced or transmitted in any form or by any means, electronic or mechanical, including photocopying, recording, or by any information storage and retrieval system, without the written permission of Beyond Words Publishing, Inc., except where permitted by law.

Editor: Julie Steigerwaldt
Managing Editor: Beth Caldwell Hoyt
Proofreader: Jade Chan
Cover Design: Laurie Dolphin
Cover Photographer: Laurent Elie Badessi
Interior Design: Jerry Soga
Composition: William H. Brunson Typography Services

Printed in the United States of America
Distributed to the book trade by Publishers Group West

Library of Congress Control Number: 2004101183

The corporate mission of Beyond Words Publishing, Inc.:
Inspire to Integrity

For

Carley, Jeremy, David, and Holly.

and

To the memory of

Sally Anne Stuart Forbes (1921–1999)

and

Agnes (Gibson) Willoughby Hodgson (1860–1949),

artful spirits who inspire from beyond.

The challenge is not to simplify life,

but to simply live.

CONTENTS

Section One: **Physical Clutter**

The possessions in our world that do not have a purpose, do not reflect who we are, and do not enhance our lives aesthetically or spiritually.

Section Two: **Mental Clutter**

Expectations, distractions, and obligations that affect our peace of mind.

Section Three: **Emotional Clutter**

Unfulfilling activities and the self-defeating thoughts and feelings
that keep us from our highest potential.

Epilogue: **The Uncluttered Life**

PREFACE

"A place for everything, and everything all over the place."
—Steve Pridgeon, writer

We nearly lost the battle.

My husband, Bob, and I were poised to spend ten years' worth of vacation funds toward enlarging our house. The spoils of the Good Life had infiltrated the nooks and crannies of our home and taken charge. Clothes spilled from closets. Sports and camping gear, an army of linens, gardening paraphernalia, and the bits and pieces of two lifetimes were crowding us out.

But it wasn't just *stuff* invading our world. There was too much of everything. We sandwiched jobs, family, friends, meetings, volunteering, home duties, and gardening into our frenetic lives. "God" became a word to express frustration and peace was a prize thwarted by the need to have it all. Yet life was fun.

For a while.

We gaily careened through our whirlwind lives until finally we lunged into spin cycle and tumbled out of control. That's when we slammed on the brakes. Somehow our stuff, along with the daily hassles and spiritual minefields in our grab-and-run world, had squeezed us out. It wasn't just the stuff around us that brought claustrophobic feelings but also invasive technology, information anxiety, nuisance noise, deadlines, decisions, and an overload of expectations. Negative feelings, toxic people, resentments, and worries created confusion. Somehow it all ended up on the kitchen table of life. Inside and out, clutter plagued us and threatened to control us.

Rather than earmark future earnings to build more room to house more stuff, we decided to take charge and cull what mattered from what didn't. We yearned for a home that sheltered us from the hurly-burly. We wanted a life that reflected our deepest desires. The simple life was not our goal; we just wanted a less complicated one. We wanted more time for each other and those we love. So we pledged to separate what we really needed from what we thought we needed. But we didn't want to abandon our comforts to take up a Walden-like existence—we liked our comfortable life. So where to begin?

William Morris, father of the British Arts and Crafts Movement and the darling of the 1880s carriage set, offered a message that still resonates today: Have nothing in your houses that is not useful or you do not believe to be beautiful. That seemed easy enough. The steak knives and Chinese tapestry stay; so do the best two of four bikes. But the second-generation computer and eight extra backpacks go, as does stuff that's been packed away in the underwear drawers for so long it could inspire a career in archeology. And the trophy head of the Rocky Mountain goat Bob shot twenty years ago—beautiful? I think not! But that poor goat head still captivates Bob (it must be those big, brown, glassy eyes), so we retreated to negotiate that matter another day.

A painting bought on a whim twelve years ago—a constant reminder that I'd dropped too much cash on something I didn't love then and don't hang now—stirred regret, not joy. I slated that for auction. A bundle of faded hydrangeas from last year's bloom lacked the appeal of the real thing. They went, too. We continued to ruthlessly attack the storage areas, bedrooms, and especially the garage, the holdall for hard-core clutter. It took much longer than we had expected, but we stood our ground and even gained some, especially when I dumped fourteen pairs of out-of-date shoes.

But our stuff is fertile—it reproduced overnight. Before the year was out, the house was clogged again. Feng shui expert Beth Skala suggested that we determine why we were tossing each item. "Is it something new we want in its place, or just clean, clear space? If you don't make the choice, your subconscious makes it for you. Often that means replacing it with exactly the same thing."

Aha, so that explains the seven pairs of new shoes—bought on sale, of course—crowded at the back of my closet.

Clutter also tells secrets. Denise Linn, author of *Feng Shui for the Soul*, wrote that a person's possessions and how they are arranged reveals more than any résumé. Our homes and work-places contain encoded information about us. The pictures we hang, the books on our shelves, and the music we play reveal clues about us. They can also be metaphors for what we desire. Model airplanes decorating a banker's office could indicate that he'd rather be zooming over the Pacific. The teacher who ani-mates her classroom with travel posters reveals an adventurous wanderlust. And Bob's goat head? Hmmm.

With all this to consider, Bob and I replaced our haphazard interest to clear clutter with a renewed urge to purge. This time we devised a strategy. We'd chop the job into small bits: one room at a time, or if pressed for time, we'd tackle just a single drawer or closet. First, we attacked the kitchen.

Miles Davis crooned in the background as we downed a wee dram of Scotland's finest to kick-start the event. Out came a box marked "Yard Sale," another labeled "Charity," and a third we called "Undecided." Into the Yard Sale box went once-used quiche dishes. (*Ouch!*) Then followed a heart-shaped cake pan bought when the kids were small and two of the three can openers we owned. "I didn't know I needed this until I saw it," Bob said with a laugh, as he set a still-packaged electric knife into the Yard Sale box. I added fancy ice-cube molds, paper towel holders, and a hard-boiled egg slicer. The box soon swelled with discards.

As we continued to unclutter, we realized that our stuff was loaded with memories. Chucking the grungy frying pan Bob had taken camping in the years before mortgages and kids seemed like a logical move—to me. But parting with my pinwheel crystal sugar bowl, despite the fact that its lid was missing, was another matter. After a few tussles, we agreed we'd put some things aside for a second look another time.

We discovered that battling clutter isn't a one-time thing but a continuous process. It requires a shift from impulsive acquisition to being mindful about what we bring into our home, minds, and hearts. It means pitching what doesn't serve us and enhancing our lives to make room for what does. Most importantly, remaining uncluttered means examining our relationship with our stuff.

Living and working among useful, beautiful, or spiritually enhancing objects help make life productive and joyful. Letting go of negative emotions is just as important. Technology overload, environmental annoyances, money issues, time stress, guilt, resentments, and worry all clutter our lives just as piles of newspapers or packed attics do.

You won't find all the culprits here, nor will you find all the answers, for your clutter is tailor-made. But *Unclutter Your Life* will inspire you to take control of your outer and inner environments. Like Monday morning washing, battling clutter is an ongoing challenge that can be mastered, and the payoff is a vibrant life filled with purpose, zest, and happiness.

This book contains twenty chapters of short, lively narratives divided into three sections: Physical Clutter, Mental Clutter, and Emotional Clutter. Each chapter identifies a single clutter culprit and presents ideas and solutions culled from well-known experts, friends, and my own experience. At the end of every chapter you'll find a list of Clutter Busters that provides additional concrete strategies to wrestle that particular clutter demon. Resource books, organizations, and Web sites are listed at the end of the book in a handy Resources section.

Through sharing what I've learned in *Unclutter Your Life* I hope to inspire you to address the daily hassles that can fragment life. When we attack clutter with action, clarity, and a good spring-cleaning, creative potential is unleashed. This is my wish for you.

Live clutter-free,

K.G.

Victoria, Canada

2004

ACKNOWLEDGEMENTS

This book reflects the immense generosity of many. Marianne Scott's wise counsel and sharp eye helped me see when the fog rolled in. Linda Langford of Sydney, Australia, offered clear thoughts and clever suggestions. Barbara Ballard took time to read and comment. Experts in Canada, the United States, and beyond shared their knowledge. Countless others offered personal experiences. Friends infused me with encouragement over many cups of tea. Each individual added to the texture of *Unclutter Your Life* and made writing it a joy. My appreciation to you all goes beyond words.

I thank my agent, Carolyn Swayze, for connecting me with the angels at Beyond Words Publishing. With editor-in-chief Cynthia Black at the helm, I could not have asked for a more committed and talented team.

A special thank you to my son, David, who agreed to give up television. That decision sparked the story, "Unplugged," that inspired *Unclutter Your Life*.

I am forever grateful to my mother, Kay Gibson, who launched my love affair with words by encouraging me to read as soon as I could hold a book. She sets the standard for initiative and perseverance.

And a lifetime of hugs to Bob Unwin, my husband and my first editor, who said, "Just do it."

Note:

In some cases, the names of people referred to by first name have been changed to protect their privacy.

Any errors or omissions are the author's alone.

SECTION ONE
Physical Clutter

The possessions in our world that do not have a purpose, do not reflect who we are, and do not enhance our lives aesthetically or spiritually.

CHAPTER 1

Clutter: Trash or Treasures?

"Surely, there must be more to life than having everything."
—Maurice Sendak, author

Even though my husband and I continually purge clutter from our home, we admit an awful truth: we'll always be pack rats. I still find odd bits of string, screws, pens, flashlights, dog biscuits, and grocery coupons crammed into drawers. We still tell ourselves that those extra boots might come in handy someday and that the kids might want our extra camping gear. Bob is convinced that we should keep those empty bottles just in case we decide to craft our own wine. I still hoard unused picture frames.

Clutter is a personal made-to-measure sort of problem. But surely there's a defining standard, a "clutter rule" of sorts. According to *The Oxford Dictionary of Current English*, clutter is "a crowded and untidy collection of things." In her book, *Clear Your Clutter with Feng Shui*, Karen Kingston defined clutter as "things we don't use or love, too many things in small spaces, and anything unfinished." Clutter also extends beyond the physical and into our emotional and spiritual well-being, surfacing in negative, life-limiting thoughts; relationships with toxic people; and disruptive or abusive situations.

Clutter affects how we feel. It shows no mercy as it clouds life with anxiety and frustration. The chaos that clutter creates can make us feel overwhelmed and defeated. It creates tension in relationships when things become lost or misplaced. Clutter eats up time as we search for shoes, keys, and lunch bags and it creates work as we shop for, clean, and manage our stuff. It costs us money as we insure, repair, and transport our precious goods and replace things we can't find.

And clutter devours space. A survey by Royal Lepage, a Canadian realty company, indicated that six out of ten homeowners have garages and two-thirds of those are so crammed with clutter that the cars lose out.

So why do we clutter? Christy Best, a California-based professional organizer, said that we often don't critically consider what comes into our homes. "Clutter just happens. Often the 'just-in-case' excuse is at work." I know what Ms. Best means. When Bob and I attacked our kitchen clutter we found multiple bottle openers, enough drink coasters to host the National Rugby Team, and knives we didn't know we owned. "Keep a few items, but not a lifetime's worth," Ms. Best said. "If you let go of something you're later in need of, chances are you'll find a replacement."

Karla Jones, a professional organizer in San Mateo, California, said that nostalgia also breeds clutter. "I know pack rats with cartons of souvenirs from trips they took thirty years ago. Others have programs from every concert they've attended and boxes stuffed with remnants of their childhoods, past careers, and love affairs. Holding on to these things keeps us in the past. We can strain our necks looking back." Ms. Jones suggested that we keep a few tokens and let the rest go. "Why live with memories when every day holds new adventures? That's where the richness of life is."

What else drives the need to acquire and keep on acquiring? The love of things plagues pack rats who can't resist the urge to buy more than they can use. "I've seen homes packed with new purchases—some still are in their shopping bags," said Ms. Jones. For some, acquiring provides a sense of abundance. Like cozy feather comforters, possessions can give us a sense of belonging and a measure of status. With stuff around us, we feel lathered in prosperity and self-worth. Homes knee-deep in Sale Day clutter might ease a poverty mentality. But according to Noble Peace Prize winner Mahatma Gandhi, abundance is a state of mind— and accessible to everyone. He said that it flourishes not when we grasp and hoard but when we release what no longer serves us and open our lives to others.

An overabundance of material possessions might provide a barrier between ourselves and our feelings. Shopping provides a welcome diversion from dealing with life's issues, especially painful ones. And as more stuff comes into our lives, it takes more time to organize, keeping us occupied and safely insulated from the outside world.

Clutter can be a way to send messages to others. Books, coats, shoes, school assignments, and the like trailing behind a teenager might signal her need for more personal space or power in the family. An overflowing office might tell clients we're too busy for them or lead our bosses to pass us over for new projects. And who can entertain or host guests in a messy house?

Sometimes we hang on to stuff to honor the past. I once visited a home that was quite beautiful. Its large, graceful rooms were filled with family heirlooms, many dating back to the nineteenth century. But to the woman who lived there, they were pure clutter. "These things are clearly valuable," she said, "but they don't reflect who I am or the life I want to lead. They keep me stuck. I feel like I'm trapped in someone else's life, yet I keep these things because I feel I have to."

Then there are the collectors. Are they hoarding trash or harboring treasures? Michael Thompkins, a cognitive behavioral therapist in San Francisco, suggests that genuine collectors have a vision. "Legitimate collections have value and meaning. They are ordered and reflect a purpose. Collectors research and seek out particular objects. They exercise skill and knowledge. Pack rats keep everything—and lots of it."

I once saw an amazing display of model commercial airplanes at the Great Falls, Montana airport. Barry Poletto began building this fleet as a hobby that is now thought to be the most extensive of its kind—too extensive for Barry's home. "I probably have more than a thousand planes. I research and design each one to look exactly like the original." He gave the collection to the airport when it outgrew the house. "I'm still making planes," he confessed, "and it's great to know that because they are out in the public, others enjoy them, too."

Too many things create chaos and confusion. Feng shui experts agree that clutter stagnates *chi*, the energy that breathes life into our homes and offices. When chi is blocked, it creates imbalance. Chi wants to move freely through hallways and rooms, and it loves sun, fresh air, and unobstructed space. Carolyn, a freelance editor who lives in a small, one-bedroom apartment that doubles as her office, understands the importance of chi. Her home, though compact, has a spacious air. Carolyn has perfected the art of anti-clutter. She can find her keys in a flash and she knows what's in each file folder. She has just enough of everything. Even though Carolyn's life buzzes with everyday demands, she exudes a thoughtful, unhurried rhythm. Like her home, she is composed and relaxed. "I try to keep things flowing, releasing what I no longer need. For me there is joy in letting things go— knowing that someone else will use them. This contributes to harmony in my life and creates quiet in my mind and body."

Clutter is capricious. It moves effortlessly from the physical world into our mental, emotional, and spiritual realms. But when we purge physical clutter, mental clutter goes with it and life becomes smoother and less frantic. With less clutter, Bob and I have more room for what really matters and some to spare. While we still have much to learn, we're clear on a few important points:

- ☐ Our possessions should be useful or, in our mind, beautiful.
- ☐ Our possessions should enhance our physical, emotional, and spiritual environments.
- ☐ Clutter sends messages and tells secrets.
- ☐ Clutter can block opportunities by telling others we are disorganized or incapable.
- ☐ Attachments to old stuff keep us from new pleasures.
- ☐ Clearing clutter is a continual process.

- ☐ **Start immediately by not adding to your possessions. Resist bringing anything into your home that does not have a purpose, inspire you, or spiritually enhance your life.**

- ☐ **Assess your priorities. The love of things can overshadow the love of life and people. Beware of nostalgia; things are just things.**

- ☐ **Let go of guilt. Gifts you do not use and expensive mistakes can be clutter, too. Give them to others who can use and appreciate them.**

- ☐ **Visualize the calm and in-control feeling clear space gives. I often flip through Jane Tidbury's wonderful book *Zen Style: Balance and Simplicity for Your Home* to remind me of uncluttered rooms that exude peace and serenity.**

- ☐ **Unclutter first, then organize—or you may fall into the trap of organizing clutter.**

- ☐ **Analyze your pack-rat habits. Assess everything you haven't used within the past year. Don't overlook attics and storage cupboards.**

- ☐ **Designate boxes for trash, charity, give away, yard sale, and consignment and put them in an accessible spot.**

- ☐ **Begin with the obvious. Discard broken toys, unused appliances, outdated newspapers, magazines and brochures, orphaned shoes and gloves, and take-out food containers.**

- [ ] Attack one room at a time. Remove everything from each cupboard, closet, drawer, and shelf. Assess each item with these questions:
  - When did I last use this?
  - Is it outdated?
  - Is it still relevant in my life?
  - Does it make me feel good?
  - Do I have more than one?
  - Do I really need it? Why?
  - Will my life change if I let this go?

- [ ] Keep just those items that have a definite purpose. Designate an undecided box for the maybes.

- [ ] Every item needs a proper and logical home. Objects in the wrong place become clutter magnets. Remove stuff from the floors, under furniture, and behind doors.

- [ ] Dispose of your clutter immediately. Otherwise it will creep back in.

- [ ] Take time each day to unclutter, even if it's just while the tea is steeping. Uncluttering a single kitchen drawer, a shelf in a bedroom, or the closet can take just a few minutes. So does going through your purse or wallet, cleaning out the trunk of the car, or gathering outdated newspapers and magazines.

- [ ] If the process of uncluttering overwhelms you, get help. See Resources for professional organizers in your area.

2

Closet Clutter

"Getting rid of old clothes is like shedding old skin."
—Carol Hathaway, psychologist

Wardrobe consultant Shai Thompson peered into my crammed-to-the-hilt closet. It resembled a magician's trunk—eclectic, colorful, and full of multiple personalities—and it overwhelmed me. While there was plenty in my closet, I often felt as though I had little to wear. Rather than rummaging through all my stuff, I would grab the old usuals and throw them on. Stuff I hadn't worn in ages jostled for space with well-loved regulars. It wasn't that I suffered from shop-till-you-drop syndrome, nor did I prowl the malls when life demanded a diversion. I just didn't throw anything out, and I couldn't resist digging for treasures in consignment stores. As never-ending bargains jammed my closet, my clothes and my mind swirled in a frenzy of confusion.

My savvy stepdaughter, Holly, had tried to help. "You gotta know the difference between fashion and fad. Some things are just for one season. Buy them cheap, and when they aren't fun any-more, out they go. Don't hang on to them," this fountain of twenty-something wisdom had said. "Sure, styles might return—like the bell-bottom jeans you guys wore in the seventies—but when they do, it's with a twist. You just can't fake fashion. Trust me."

I did. At least that's what I'd told her.

Yet I still owned suits that had lost their cachet a decade ago. And there were things I didn't wear because I couldn't—like the hip-hugging skirt that was snug when I'd bought it and impossi-ble to squeeze into now. But because it was *sooo* beautiful it sat, tucked away on a shelf, wrapped in layers of guilt, two sizes too small, two decades later.

Hopefully Shai would make sense of it all. I saluted her as she charged into my closet. Her mission seemed simple enough: remove the clutter and make a working wardrobe from what's left. Secretly, I doubted it was possible. Can anyone make sense of thirty-four shirts, a rack of black pants, sweaters that dated to the Nixon era (I'm telling no lies here), twenty-seven pairs of shoes, jackets and coats, more pants, and special occasion dresses that had seen their day? If she could, Shai was a miracle worker.

It turned out that she was.

It was daunting to let Shai into my closet, for clothes are very personal. Closets reveal our history, personality, and fantasies. But Shai was gentle. One by one, she took each piece and gave it the once-over. "When did you last use this?" she queried, holding up a fencing mask from my freshman year. I gave her a pained look. "And this?" referring to a rainbow-colored batik jacket bought at a street market in my hippy-dippy days. "I can't quite see you in these anymore," she said, pulling a pair of red spiked heels from the jumble on the closet floor.

"Nice piece," she commented, retrieving a silky, mustard-colored thing from the far-reaches of the closet, "but definitely not your color. Don't wear it much, do you?" She was oh so right! According to Shai, at least 80 percent of our clothes just hang. She zeroed in on the reason. "Although we buy clothes for all sorts of reasons, we instinctively wear what makes us feel good," she said. "And mustard, darling, is simply not you."

Orphans without a thing to go with them, clothes that didn't fit, and others that belonged to dimly remembered decades surfaced. My bed disappeared under growing piles of out-of-season outfits, total discards, and sentimental hangers-on. Among the rumpled heaps lay a load of freeloaders—clothes I had forgotten I owned. On one lonely corner lay a much smaller keep-it heap. Eventually the closet was bare.

Before Shai assessed the clothes that still had potential, we talked about the life I led that was different from the one before. Because I worked at home, I didn't need business gear other than a few pieces for meeting clients, leading a seminar, or speaking to a group. On weekends I was more likely to shuffle into a foreign movie than to shake my booty at a downtown club. Comfy, casual, and easy care—that was for me.

When Shai finished working her magic, I gasped. We had four huge bags for charity and a smaller lot for consignment. The pieces that had survived Shai's scrutiny were back in the closet, hung according to color. They looked lonely. It struck me as unnatural—just plain strange—to see space between hangers.

With great effort, I resisted the compulsion to fill those gaps. As the weeks passed, my spending plummeted as I consciously considered each purchase. (Does it go with anything? Do I really need this? Do I have others just like it? Would I buy it if it weren't on sale?) There were other benefits. I saved time cleaning and organizing and, with only clothes I actually wear hanging on the rack, I didn't agonize over what to wear. Life's ship sailed a little more smoothly.

But clothes clutter is more than dowdy dinosaurs and too-snug skirts. Sentimental clothing lurks in many closets. Memories of triumphs, disappointments, and hopes are embedded in T-shirts from special events, outdated dresses, and ya-ya getups. They sit and stagnate like forgotten yearbooks and tarnished sports trophies. "Keep the memories," Shai said. "As for the clothes, well, they're just clothes."

Until Shai stepped in, my friend Jessica agonized over a closet filled with emotional attachments. Next to a naughty little black number and well-loved jeans hung hand-tailored silk shirts, exquisite ties, and a vest—all clothes that had belonged to her deceased father. "I keep Dad's things as a way of hanging on to him," Jessica explained. She wasn't alone. Favorite garments that once belonged to someone dear help connect us to their essence, their presence.

"Why not keep a few items and actually use them?" Shai suggested. She showed Jessica how to convert her father's hand-woven tie into a little purse and one of his silk shirts into a pillow cover. Later Jessica transferred a family picture onto it. "Instead of a useless shirt in the closet, I have a memento I look at every day. As for Dad's vest, I wear it; it's great with jeans."

Contented, Jessica was able to say good-bye to the rest of her father's things. Inspired to use rather than just pack away sentimental possessions, Jessica also rescued a collection of evening bags stashed away on her top shelf. "These belonged to my mother," she said of the little beaded bags and delicate velvet purses with rhinestone clasps. "They remind me of Mom's elegant days of gala balls and opera openings. They're so beautiful. I'm going to display all of them." And when Jessica stepped out, they would make a terrific accent to her ensemble.

Clothes clutter is not just a girl thing. In his book *Men of Style*, Donald C. Richardson cautions men not to buy stuff just because it's on sale or because they plan to lose a few pounds. If it doesn't fit now, forget it. Christy Best adds that men often clutter their closets with old clothes put aside for gardening, fishing, and messy chores. "Trouble is, they keep far too much," she said. "One outfit is usually enough."

Fashion retailer Colleen Gibson buys three or four mix-and-match outfits each spring. "In September I give them away and purchase a handful of cold-weather outfits," she said. "I wear only white and black. That's it. There's no confusion in my closet, and because I buy new clothes each season, my look is current." Colleen combines practicality with frugality and comes out looking smashing.

Like Jessica and Colleen, I came to understand that uncluttering our closets is not just about clothes. It's about clarity—in our physical surrounding and in our minds. As Shai and I worked through my closet, I carted away years of internal clutter embedded in the discards. It was not only a physical purge but a way for me to gain enormous psychological peace. I felt uplifted, clearer, and calmer.

We lose more than our clutter when we purge the closet. Gone are the confusion and inner battles that infuse the start of the day. Gone is the guilt over buying expensive, unworn mistakes. And gone are the negative body image messages woven into clothes that no longer fit.

I realized that fueled by the media with its incessant mantra of materialism, we often confuse need with desire. I also recognized the absurdity of our middle-class expectations. How often do good moods and bad ones, a friend's birthday, or a surprise sale kick-start a trip to the mall? And what about shopping for entertainment or as a release from boredom?

Now when the gray skies drag me down (and we have plenty of those here in the Pacific Northwest), I disappear into a book or meet a friend for coffee and a chat.

And I'm winning the battle . . . most of the time! While I've become a more thoughtful shopper, I am still tempted to wander into stores and linger over beautiful things. Sometimes I put my money down, but I'm more likely to pause to consider whether that cute pair of strappy sandals on sale at a ridiculously great price really has a purpose in my life or if they will just become more clutter.

One thing is for certain: My closet has far less in it, and surprisingly, I have more to wear.

So I think I'll pass on those cute little sandals.

This time, anyway.

CLUTTER BUSTERS

☐ **Avoid storage bins and organizers. If your closets and drawers are overflowing, you have too much stuff and it's time to unclutter. Get a clutter buddy, or, for the price of a good pair of shoes, hire a wardrobe consultant or a professional organizer. Clothing stores can recommend a specialist.**

☐ **Take a realistic look at your life. Events such as a new job or a move to a new community will influence what we wear and what stagnates in the closet. Consider how you spend your leisure time. Does your job require you to meet the public? Do you work at home? Have you retired or become a parent? Let your closet reflect your current lifestyle.**

☐ **Make a date with your closet.**

☐ **Take everything out, one piece at a time.**

☐ **Place orphaned, out-of-date, and poor-fitting clothes into boxes for charity or consignment or to give away.**

☐ **Put keepers in a separate pile. These are clothes that are current and make you feel terrific.**

☐ **Analyze the keepers. Are there pieces that don't coordinate with others? If so, chances are that they are rarely, if ever, worn. These are candidates for consignment.**

☐ Separate, clean, and store out-of-season clothes in breathable containers away from those in current use.

☐ Set aside pieces that need cleaning or repair for immediate attention.

☐ Discard scuffed and outdated shoes. Experts say we often reach for the same two or three comfortable pairs.

☐ Two purses are often enough.

☐ We often discover non-clothes items in the closet. Put them where they belong.

☐ Consider creative uses for sentimental clothing. Recycle material from wedding dresses into christening gowns. Floor-length dresses can be shortened. Clothes made from beautiful material can be recast as pillow covers or place mats for special occasions.

☐ Install hooks in your closet for belts, scarves, and purses.

☐ Remember to unclutter your drawers with the same criteria as for your closet. Be ruthless with underwear and socks.

3

The Essential Traveler

"Remember, in your travels you'll meet two kinds of tourists—
those who pack light and those who wish they had."
—Rick Steves, travel guru

Weeks before catching the 747, I meticulously organized a wardrobe for a journey through Europe. It was my first trip overseas and I was ready for every possible situation—or so I'd thought. Oversized suitcases held things I considered essential. It took the quick fingers of Barcelonan thieves to show me just how unnecessary most of it was. Thanks to their handiwork, everything I had packed disappeared in minutes.

Regrets? Just one: I wish they'd done it sooner.

The day began with anticipation as I motored from France, over the Pyrenees, and into Spain. I'd spent two weeks immersed in the splendor of French vineyards, explored historic châteaux, and gorged on the local cheeses. While France was divine, the promise of authentic paella spurred me toward Barcelona. When I arrived, I was eager to dive into the dizzy world of Catalonian culture, but first I needed a room. As I passed quirky museums devoted to footwear collections, funeral carriages, and bull fighting, a small budget hotel, crammed amongst merchant shops near the harbor, caught my eye.

I cautiously parked my rented Fiat near the entrance, ducked inside, and negotiated a three-day stay. As a final assurance, I scrambled up two flights of stairs to inspect the room for uninvited critters known to freeload in shabby waterfront hostelries. In the few minutes it took me to give the room the once-over, my travel experiences were altered forever. While I peered under the bed and inside the closet, my little car, locked and clearly visible, was having an adventure with Barcelona's darker side.

In the time it takes to click a castanet, thieves pried open the trunk and helped themselves. A gathering of regulars at a nearby café, experts in the fine art of people watching, observed the drama. "What could we do?" the onlookers said with unconvincing looks of helplessness.

Now what was I to do? I had nothing but the clothes I was wearing. I fumed as I visualized my skirts and tops (with matching shoes and purses, of course), short and long pants, coordinating sweaters and jackets, belts, jewelry, and scarves up for sale at a backstreet flea market.

The next day, I felt surprisingly elated and free. I had been reborn as a new-age minimalist. I purchased one small duffle bag and then sought out a *très petit* ensemble. "Essential" had taken on a new meaning. I realized that it had been a huge strain lugging my stuff up and down hotel stairs and in and out of the car, not to mention schlepping it around train stations and through crowded airports. Other than my toothbrush, I didn't miss a thing. My burden had, quite simply, disappeared, and I didn't want it back. Those nimble-fingered entrepreneurs were my saviors, my heroes! I'd kiss them if I could.

Losing my luggage significantly influenced the rest of trip and the others that followed. By traveling with only what I could carry, I didn't fear a second go-round with thieves; there wasn't much to tempt them. Choosing what to wear each day was as easy as putting on what I had rinsed out the night before, and I was relieved of heave-hoeing my middle-class identity around Europe. Best of all, the distraction of all that stuff—my travel clutter—was gone.

I had the chance to test my resolve when I took up travel writing. When Bob joined me for a month-long cycling tour of Holland, we opted for two pairs of pants each (one pair for the plane; the other had zip-off legs to become shorts), four T-shirts, and a rainproof jacket. Bicycling shorts, a light sweater, socks, and minimal underwear rounded out our wardrobes. Everything had to pass the lightweight, quick-dry test. As for toiletries, we shared toothpaste and sunscreen and kept the rest to a minimum. I'll admit that our appearance did little to inspire a fashion state-ment, and we were sick to death of every garment by the end of the trip, but we could pack and unpack in minutes and the whole lot weighed less than a round of Gouda. As for souvenirs and gifts, we shipped them home as soon as possible.

During another adventure, we scooted around Britain with just carry-on bags. On arriving at Heathrow, we strolled off a too-long flight, bag in hand, breezed through customs, and were out the door while the uninformed hung back at the carousel, hoping their luggage wasn't on its way to Hamburg.

But there's more to conquering travel clutter than packing light. We learned to pack less into our itinerary. Snap-and-dash trips, weighed down with lists of must-dos, smother the serendipity that gives travel its magic. Attempting to discover each and every attraction of a place reduces travel to a dizzy kaleidoscope of superficial experiences. Defining moments are found in even the tiniest place if we make the time.

One of my fondest assignments involved a trip to the Scottish island of Arran. A friend had warned me, "A day is all you need. Any more than that and you'll be mooing with those shaggy Highland cows." Oh, how wrong she had been. I biked on winding country lanes, discovered secluded beaches laden with gifts the tide had left behind, and savored a few pints in a countryside pub where the bartender dished out a side order of bagpipe music. I spent one entire afternoon discovering the delights of a castle garden and more time than I'll admit swapping lies with the folks who call Arran home. The memory of that trip remains as intoxicating as the island's sea-scented breeze.

Uncluttered travel is about taking less so we can bring more home. This goes beyond great photos and souvenirs to include memories of a place. I still recall the richness of a day spent on a mountain trail in Jasper, Alberta, a raging lightning storm in Montana, and the tales I heard from an old man selling newspapers in a Paris kiosk. Uncluttered travel is about traveling with our hands free and our minds, hearts, and souls wide open.

CLUTTER BUSTERS

☐ Books abound with light-packing tips but my bottom line is simple: Be ruthless. I have yet to meet anyone who moans about not having taken enough.

☐ If you can't carry it onto the plane, don't take it. Although figures vary according to the airline, on average 1 in 200 bags goes missing. Most eventually show up, but others vanish, rerouted to the eternal baggage carousel in the sky.

☐ Pick a bag that works. Travel guru and author Rick Steves devised a nylon suitcase that converts to a backpack large enough to hold gear for his three-month travel stints; it even meets most airlines' carry-on guidelines.

☐ Each item should do double or triple duty, be lightweight and easy to launder, and coordinate with absolutely everything. Consider convertible pants, anything fleece, and microfiber fabrics.

☐ Choose grime-hiding, dark-colored clothing made from fabrics that wick away perspiration, keep the body warm, don't crease, and dry overnight. Silk or stretch lace undies are light and dry quickly.

☐ Consider one pair of walking shoes and one lighter pair, such as walking sandals.

☐ Other than a plain wedding ring and a knock-off watch, I leave valuables at home.

- [ ] Pack for the purpose. If it's business, forget the Birkenstocks. If it's pleasure, forget the pinstripes.

- [ ] Clothes with pockets, especially deep ones, hold maps, gloves, tips, and telephone change. Tilley Endurables has the lead on pocket clothing.

- [ ] Wear a money belt to protect against light-fingered encounters.

- [ ] Because thefts do happen, compile a list of everything you take (handy for insurance purposes) and make two copies of essential documents, including your passport, credit cards, travel insurance, airline tickets, and trip itinerary. Leave one list with a friend and take the other with you; keep it separate from the original documents.

- [ ] Unclutter your travel plans. Plan longer stays in fewer places. Take time to wander and explore. Unexpected, serendipitous moments make the trip.

One-Bag Wonder Packing List

(I use this same list whatever the trip duration. Everything fits in a carry-on bag.)

- [ ] *1 pair pants (no-crease docker-style)

- [ ] 1 pair of pants that convert to shorts

- [ ] *1 jacket (rain-resistant, fold-into-a-pocket style)

- [ ] *1 long-sleeved T-shirt

- [ ] *1 pair walking shoes

☐   1 pair walking sandals

☐   3 quick-dry, no-iron shirts

☐   1 casual, wrinkle-free dress. (For men, a decent shirt to go with the docker pants.)

☐   1 light sweater—whatever the season or destination

☐   4 pairs underwear (quick-dry)

☐   4 pairs socks (quick-dry)

☐   1 swimsuit

☐   1 small towel

☐   1 hat

*Items I *wear on the plane.*

For cool seasons, add gloves, a scarf, and a collapsible umbrella. Fleece sweaters and pants, which come in various weights, are ideal travel choices as they are warm even if wet, lightweight, and wrinkle-resistant. Boring but versatile black is the way to go.

Miscellaneous

☐   **Essential toiletries, including sunscreen; sunglasses; liquid soap that does duty as laundry soap, shampoo, and shower gel; and a moisturizer (forget blowdryers, nail polish, and perfumes).**

☐ Medications; a copy of prescriptions, including eyeglass prescriptions; a small first-aid kit; vitamins; waterless handwash; and scissors.

☐ Four clothespins and an elastic laundry line.

☐ Passport and visa, health documentation, emergency information, medical insurance, hotel reservations, photocopies of all documentation, and just the keys needed on your arrival home.

☐ A notebook, one guidebook, camera and film, a travel alarm clock, a daypack, a money belt, and a small combination lock.

CHAPTER 4

Rainy-day Clutter

*"Find your joy in something finished,
not a thousand things begun."*
—Douglas Mallock, poet

"One hour is the limit. My bottom can't take it any longer," a dinner guest moaned. Another nodded in support. I blushed with embarrassment and topped off their wine glasses. The solid-wood chairs they sat on were a work of art—the lucky result of an afternoon spent combing second-hand stores. But I had to concede that unless my guests were well-endowed with natural padding, those chairs become a pain in the butt long before the salad was served.

It's not that I had intended to inflict discomfort on my guests. I had had noble intentions of whipping up comfy cushions when I purchased the chairs three years ago. I had even shelled out a day's pay for some terrific rose-colored silk and bags of filling. But that lovely material just sat, gathering dust along with a thin, unseen layer of guilt.

Each time I walked into the dining room, I thought about the polite but terse complaints I'd hear at the next get-together. "I'll get those cushions done," I'd tell myself. After all, they were on the list—the rainy-day list.

Unfinished projects are as haunting as bad dreams. Those cushions weren't the only projects of mine that languished in a tangle of good intentions. A partly refinished side table with oodles of potential and a jumble of unsorted photographs called for attention, along with tarnished silver and clothes with loose buttons or ripped seams. Why didn't I just get at them, enjoy the results, and rid myself of the little voice that taunted, teased, and tormented me? Those rainy-day projects, unfinished promises of great-things-to-be, cluttered more than my home; they cluttered my mind.

"Am I just lazy? A procrastinator?" I asked feng shui expert Beth Skala. "Maybe," she said with a laugh, "but it's likely something much more. Unfinished projects are pure potential. They hold promises of what might be. But unless we bring them to completion, they just take up space. They're clutter—the kind that sends negative messages that say we're incompetent, disorganized, or, yes, even lazy."

She asked me to consider what was keeping me from making those cushions. After some thought, I realized that the vision of what I wanted and my ability to create it were several sewing lessons apart. "Aha," said Ms. Skala. "You're not alone. Oftentimes we take on jobs that are too ambitious for us. We get overwhelmed and although we might get them started, we often don't finish them."

When she was first married, Ms. Skala assumed that all men knew how to fix things, yet her husband would dally as taps dripped and tiles flew off the roof. She'd prod him to attend to these annoyances and he'd put her off. Finally, she realized that her husband was not a handyman—nor did he want to be. Like many of us, he avoided failure by dodging the task. "Now I hire help or get friends to lend a hand," she said, "and the projects get done."

Sometimes we have great dreams, but we just lose interest. "I have a bedspread that I began embroidering twenty years ago," a friend admitted. "I can't see myself finishing it. My interests have changed so much since I started working on it." I asked why she keeps it. "I paid a bunch for it and I've invested so much time working on it. It would be wasteful to throw it out. Who knows? I might get to it one day," she answered while admitting that that scenario is unlikely.

Then there are the "shoulds." Materials for the greenhouse we plan to build clutter the garage, while inside the house, rolls of wallpaper and cans of paint stand ready to spruce up the kitchen. Like unwelcome squatters, these things not only clutter our homes but keep us off balance and uptight. And like the albatross in Coleridge's poem "The Rime of the Ancient Mariner," these rainy-day projects get heavier and nastier the longer they hang around.

And we don't do some projects because we simply don't want to. Bob and I have the odd tussle when it's time to clean the garage. And thoughts of organizing the storage room and mending and ironing clothes put me in a nasty mood. So, of course, I do other things. It's easy to delude ourselves into thinking we're productive when we're actually stalling. We can avoid some tasks by replacing them with others that we tell ourselves are useful—like surfing the Net instead of completing a presentation or mending the rain gutters.

Emma, a friend who wanted to learn watercolor painting, spent a truckload of cash on supplies only to find—as she put it—"as an artist, I suck." That was several years ago, but Emma still has a cupboard filled with brushes, paper, and paints. Like my wannabe cushions, her art materials shoot back little messages of incompetence. "And that's why it's clutter," Ms. Skala emphasized. "Those projects nag us—make the cushions, paint a picture—but you resist. The materials hog space and the undone project unsettles the mind."

Guilt and anxiety can be motivating, though. When it's strong enough, we act. Ms. Skala suggested that we make a plan and stick to it. "Decide if the project is one you really want to do. If so, set aside time to complete it—start to finish. Then take on another. One at a time, that's the trick. You'll feel lighter and happier."

"We might feel it's weak or extravagant to pay others to do things for us," Ms. Skala said, "but why not delegate the job, swap projects with a friend, or, if you can afford it, hire help. It feels so good to get those jobs finished and off your back."

We can also inject new life into our unfinished projects by gifting them to others. Instead of my friend's bedspread languishing in a storage box, she could offer it to the folks at a senior center or to a women's church group to complete or sell at its next fundraising bazaar.

I looked at my pile of rainy-day clutter taunting me. If it disappeared, I'd be relieved, I thought. I wondered if I should pack it up and be rid of it, but instead I decided to evaluate how important each project was. It became clear that I didn't have to mend clothes I don't like or restore a table I wouldn't use. I thought of my definition of clutter: objects that are not useful, beautiful, or spiritually enhancing. These objects include the projects we've lost interest in and those that no longer reflect who we are or our current interests or lifestyle. By letting them go, we free up our physical space and end the frustrations that haunt our internal world. Room opens for new opportunities. Best of all, we empower ourselves by exerting control over our lives.

It's like those cushions: I relished the idea of having them but not of sewing them. Finally, I hired a friend to make them and now my guests enjoy dinner in comfort. Now when I top off their wine glasses, it's not because I feel guilty but because we're having a good time—right down to the seat of our pants.

CLUTTER BUSTERS

☐ **Analyze:**
- ○ **Examine your basket of projects. Ask if your unfinished projects truly have a place in your life. Discard what you can.**

☐ **Prioritize:**
- ○ **Separate the wants from the shoulds.**
- ○ **Make time for projects that give you pleasure.**

☐ **Commit:**
- ○ **Set dates to start and finish by.**
- ○ **Assess the time, materials, and skills needed for each task.**
- ○ **Give the less complicated tasks top billing.**

☐ **Action:**
- ○ **Just do it. Put on the music and have fun. Reward yourself along the way.**
- ○ **Divide large or multifaceted projects into separate tasks.**
- ○ **Swap services with a friend.**
- ○ **Hire out projects you don't want to do.**
- ○ **Resist the pull of procrastination. Stick to the task and surf the Net later.**

Office Overload

"Lawren's studio . . . is a place to invite the soul to come and gather the riches of thought, and to ponder over them, and try to express them. It is an orderly place for an orderly mind."
—Emily Carr, painter and writer, describing the studio of painter Lawren Harris in *Hundreds and Thousands*

There was a time when my home office was chaos central. If I were in the midst of a major project, event plans and speeches littered the desk and carpeted the floor. And somewhere among the confusion were notes for travel articles I hoped to write. Pictures of my kids, reference books, a half dozen coffee cups, notepads, staplers, a radio, and stacks of compact discs lay jumbled among current and completed projects. New piles spawned with each new contract. I considered buying more shelf space, extra storage bins, and nifty organizers, but then I paused. I didn't need more space. I needed less stuff.

I put my office clutter on notice and the following Saturday I unplugged the phone, turned up the music, and went to work. By noon, I had recycled box after box of files. I had bags of papers, too. I continued with fury over the next few months and as I did, I felt like I'd lost twenty stubborn pounds. The mild undercurrent of panic I lived with, but had not noticed, disappeared. As I cleared my clutter, calmness flooded in—not just into the office but into my life.

Office slobs have trademark habits. "Generally, paper is everywhere. Look for in-boxes overflowing with last year's junk mail," said professional organizer Margaret Miller. "Seriously, in-boxes are a dead giveaway; so are piles of unopened mail. I've seen desktops so buried that the only place to work is on top of the paper!"

"Is an untidy-looking office always a cluttered office?" my accountant asked me, pointing to stacks of files sitting on tables near her desk. It was tax time, her most frantic season, and clients were storming the drawbridge.

"If it's a working mess and makes sense to you, you're off the hook," I assured her. The same is true for the creative types who lay projects on the floor, spread them over the desk, or paste them to the walls. Like more than 70 percent of us, they learn and work best with visual stimulation and need to see the elements of a project to rouse the muses. Once the task is complete, however, it's time to file what's important and dump the rest. That leaves clear space (mentally and physically) for the next project.

Studies show that people who work in disorganized spaces spend up to eight hours a week looking for things or being distracted by them. Efficiency drops and stress levels rise. Credenzas and file drawers may not contain a thing in them, yet piles of paper are heaped on top of them. Some offices are so crammed with stuff that it's difficult to walk through them, let alone find a space that's not groaning under coats, old lunch bags, convention freebies, and last month's newspapers. The phone is, well, somewhere, as are the profits.

Earnings are often hidden among misplaced invoices, receipts gone astray, customer billings yet to be mailed, and lost telephone messages from clients who want to do business. I discovered firsthand how disorder can bury profits when I was on a trip to Wales. I was looking for the entrance to a Roman tunnel said to lie under a present-day wine shop in the older section of a seaside town. After finding my target and securing permission from the proprietor to the visit the cellars below the store, I headed for the basement stairs at the back of the shop. Upon descending into the cool relief of the cellars, I gazed at a scene straight out of a Gothic thriller. Musty air filled the dank passageways that opened to cobwebbed galleries crammed with crates from across Europe. Eons of grime and dust shrouded the sturdy oak tasting tables.

As I wandered around the chambers, I stumbled upon case after case of wine. According to their label dates and the thickness of the dust that covered them, they must have been delivered and then forgotten. Packing slips and inventory papers lay here and there. Clutter lay all around me—along with potential profit. As I nosed about, I drooled over vintages that could demand a small ransom. I wondered if the proprietors were aware of the revenue languishing in these corridors?

The appearance of a workplace mirrors its priorities, affecting its professional image and levels of success. "We unknowingly assess people by what surrounds them. You'd probably think twice about dealing with a lawyer whose office reflected confusion," said feng shui practitioner Lori Beardmore. "The ideal workplace should exude a positive, calm, and confident atmosphere that is congruent with who we are and what we want to achieve." She suggested that feng shui practices and symbols can help activate that success. While not everyone wants to redesign his or her life to incorporate a feng shui philosophy, subtle elements such as flowers or plants energize space, adding a touch of calm. Soft music camouflages the wheeze of the computer. A clean, bright environment is energizing.

While office clutter can affect the bottom line, it also affects our health. Working in a disorderly environment fractures our focus and creates stress, frustration, and anxiety. "Headaches, stomach problems, and neck and shoulder strain seem more common to those who work in chaos," Ms. Beardmore remarked. "There's no doubt that people work better and are happier in an orderly environment. Clutter creates negative energy that throws us off balance and makes us feel scattered, out of control, and lethargic. It's as if every item we live with has tiny, unseen strings that connect to our inner core and draw on our energy. Subconsciously we resist working in a place that doesn't feel comfortable. I have clients who take sick days to avoid the mess at work."

A clear, uncluttered work space helps us sharpen our focus. It makes a clear statement about us and what we can accomplish. Without distractions pulling us off task and with the tools at hand, it's easier to finish what we start. Our productivity rises as our anxiety levels decrease when we know we're up-to-date and on top of the game. Instead of confusion, we'll find efficiency—and the notes from yesterday's meeting. Best of all, outer clarity frees the creative spirit.

Offices are personal spaces. They are outward expressions of their occupants and reflect their personalities and working styles. By taking control of our space and making it work for us, we increase our productivity. While clearing office clutter requires commitment and action, it's worth the effort. Who knows? As we unclutter the in-box and the bottom drawers, we might just uncover a prized bottle or two of our own.

CLUTTER BUSTERS

- ☐ Designate time outside of work hours to attack your office clutter. Follow up with shorter periods on a regular basis.

- ☐ Remove everything from drawers and shelves, assess each item, and keep only what is relevant. Be ruthless.

- ☐ Eliminate duplicate documents, brochures, and sales catalogues.

- ☐ Discard old reports, out-of-date reference books, and stale files.

- ☐ Purge out-of-office experiences, such as postcards from faraway places, golf clubs, recipe books, and material for a dress you might sew one day.

- ☐ Reduce desk material. No one needs three staplers and dozens of pens.

- ☐ Cancel junk mail immediately. (See chapter 6.)

- ☐ Give each item a logical home in a drawer or on a shelf—not on the floor, under the desk, or stacked on chairs. This also saves cleaning time.

- ☐ Attack files. Keep just those pertaining to recent and current projects. Others can be archived outside the office or shredded. (I remove outdated or duplicate papers each time I look at a file.)

☐ Clear bulletin boards regularly. Each item should be current.

☐ Postponing decisions creates clutter. Resolve to deal with all outstanding issues immediately, even if it means an occasional weekend at the office. The relief you will feel is as therapeutic as taking a vacation.

☐ Stay clutter-free. Take ten minutes each day to tidy and toss.

6

Paper Clutter: Gutenberg's Curse

> *"We spend one year of our lives looking for lost or misplaced items at home and in the office."*
> —U.S. *News & World Report*

Paper can wreak havoc as thoroughly as a Kansas tornado. Document imaging, electronic data storage fields, and virtual networks may have revolutionized information management, but our world still swirls in whirlwinds of good old-fashioned paper.

I thought I'd save big bucks (and a few trees) by perusing magazines and newspapers online and by sending e-mails. Yet while we can shoot missives through space at the click of the Send button and instantly access a phone number in Dubai, the utopian vision of a paper-reduced, time-saving era still eludes us. Since the advent of e-mail, paper use is up 40 percent as we not only read our e-mails and download information pages but then print copies. With two trillion pieces of paper generated yearly in American offices, the vision of a paperless society is just pulp fiction.

Something backfired. We're submerged in paper clutter.

According to a 1996 National Association of Professional Organizers survey, Americans are bombarded with 49,060 pieces of mail during a lifetime—one-third of which is junk mail. More than 150,000 books and 10,000 periodicals are published each year, while merchants churn out 104 catalogues per U.S. address annually.

As I sat among a slew of daily papers, a few books I have yet to read, and the monthly intake of magazines, I pondered over the plethora of paper in the techno age. A dog-eared newspaper tossed onto the nearest tabletop, letters begging response, unfiled documents and bank statements, and stacks of magazines littered my office. Where to put all this stuff? At first I considered buying more filing cabinets and more shelves. Perhaps I needed a bigger office? Then I pushed the pause button.

Why not beat Gutenberg, the inventor of the printing press, at his own game?

Despite our digital-age world, we are fascinated with paper. We need to be smarter in how we use electronic media and more aware of our default to convert digital documents to paper. Our natural tendency to read from paper defeats the purpose of electronically delivered information, while at the same time it contributes to an astonishing rise in paper use and paper clutter, domestically and in business. Yet I am not alone in preferring the morning newspaper over the online version. A real book in my hands sure beats the e-substitute. But books are my nemesis; they seem to flow into my home as often as junk mail.

But wait—certainly not all books are clutter. Favorites improve with each reading and references that speak with authority still sit in my library. So do the works of writers I admire. But many of the volumes crowding the shelves offer the superficial impact of a forgettable flick. I paid my money and enjoyed the thrill but likely won't repeat the experience. Those books are better off recycled.

Sometimes a book we own might have special meaning for someone else. While sorting through a neglected closet, I discovered a forgotten yearbook. It contained a stunning collection of photographs of my schoolmate Laurie, a promising dancer and actor. Laurie died suddenly after graduation and these pictures captured her capricious, whimsical personality. While I might glance at them on occasion, I knew it would be a much valued gift for her family, so I presented it to Laurie's mother.

"My books belonged to a person I had outgrown," explained a recently divorced and self-confessed bibliophile who had disposed of his library. "They no longer had a place in my life." Books had been this man's mistress. He'd spent long hours in their company, tenderly turning pages and devouring their mysteries. "I'd read and reread them. Eventually they turned into wallpaper. Besides," he added with a chuckle, "my new place is much smaller than the house my ex and I had. I had thought about storing them, but books should be used, not packed away." Because his books reflected a period he wanted to move beyond, they no longer had a purpose in his life. And if he truly misses his Brontë or Browning? "I'll buy another copy or pop into the library."

In a world where busyness is next to godliness, paper does more than tell the world what we know. It says we count and that what we know (or what we want others to think we know) counts. Rows of leather-bound volumes in law offices dignify and impress. Stacks of files tell clients they're dealing with a much-in-demand professional. But when paper—whether in the form of books, bills, heaps of mail, magazines, last year's Christmas cards, or unfiled documents—interferes with our sense of calm, it's clutter and it's got to go.

Who among us does not stow away love letters, photographs, kids' school projects, birthday and other special cards, or theater programs? And new occasions bring more pictures, more cards, and perhaps more love letters. Strategies for keeping such memorabilia can be as simple as making a montage of the prettiest cards and letting the others go. Designating one special box for each of your children to hold a few of their treasures helps organize their memories.

But what about photographs? It had been years since I'd rummaged through my boxes of pictures. What an adventure! With snapshots of my life spread before me, I relived the happy commotion of family gatherings, moments with school chums who have now drifted afar, crazy times in faraway places, and times when the kids were small. Each was a little treasure on its own, but all together and with the certainty of more photographs in the future, I knew I needed advice.

Armed with the notion that memories don't belong in boxes, I called Anne Barrett, a consultant who specializes in producing keepsake albums. Under her gentle tutelage, I learned how to combine photographs, letters, and other memorabilia into theme albums. I found it surprisingly easy to keep just the best pictures and discard the rest. "We might end up with twenty pictures of Aunt

Jane's birthday party, but really, all we need is the best one to remind us of the occasion," said Ms. Barrett. Photos of vacation spots can be framed and hung in a hallway gallery. Special occasion pictures can be grouped in one large frame to tell a picture story. We also have the option of scanning and storing pictures electronically.

The sudden death of a favorite aunt underlined the significance of keeping track of important documents. It took several days of rummaging through drawers and cupboards before her will surfaced. By then, funeral arrangements had been completed and family misunderstandings were brewing. How I wished she had left her intentions clearly stated in a logical place.

After that experience, I resolved to file and regularly review important information such as insurance policies, property information, warranties, investment records, birth and marriage certificates, résumés, and job references. I also pledged to regularly purge obsolete tax information and warranties that were past the stipulated legal limit.

And then there's the question of expired passports. While some of us keep them as a record of our travels, storing the current passport with those that are out-of-date can create problems. I learned this firsthand on a late September afternoon as my mother and I checked in with an airline for an international trip. That's when the clerk told us that Mom had mistakenly brought an expired passport, which she kept alongside her new one. I had to fly ahead of her while she returned home to retrieve it and missed the flight. She flew out the next day—a time-consuming and expensive mistake.

It takes a vigilant and merciless strategy to avoid Gutenberg's curse. Clearing paper clutter demands that we make choices and decisions that may have needled or even paralyzed us for years. But by clearing paper clutter and organizing our affairs, we can avoid overdue payments on bills and library books, and we save time looking for misplaced or lost documents. We will effortlessly retrieve what we need when we need it.

When Gutenberg's legacy is under control, space opens in our homes and in our minds for today's pleasures. We stop the turmoil that stirs within us when we can't find things and are rewarded with a sense of inner calm that flows from an orderly physical environment.

CLUTTER BUSTERS

☐ Resist keeping theater programs, brochures for slow-drip irrigation systems, and outdated magazines pawned off by well-meaning (and less cluttered) friends.

☐ Cancel subscriptions for newsletters, newspapers, and magazines you don't read. At the office, eliminate unnecessary product information and promotional materials.

☐ Handle paper immediately. Take action, file, or discard.

☐ If you can't find a document in less than a minute, it's in the wrong place.

☐ File, don't pile. But before you put it away, be sure it's a document you need. Sources say that 80 percent of what we file is never accessed again. Set up a system of current files, inactive files, and permanent records. Current files should include employment contracts, credit card information, insurance policies, health records, warranties, that year's bank statements, and income tax information. Inactive files contain items from old files that may have relevance. These files should be reviewed yearly. Nothing in them should be older than three years. Permanent records should be kept in a safe-deposit box to protect against fire or theft. These records include birth or death certificates, marriage or divorce papers, real estate deeds, automobile ownership papers, stocks and bonds, contracts, wills, and an inventory of household effects.

- [ ] Open mail beside the trash can or recycling box. Give bills an immediate turnaround. Try responding directly on the paper sent to you if possible.

- [ ] Recycle newspapers, newsletters, and magazines as soon as new ones arrive.

- [ ] Clip and recycle. Keep scissors handy when you read the daily papers to clip anything that requires a second look. Recycle the rest. Act on the clippings at the end of each week.

- [ ] Consider automated payment on bills or pay them directly online. Consolidate credit cards to reduce the number of bills you receive.

- [ ] Consolidate your bank accounts.

- [ ] Eliminate junk mail. (Fred Elbel of EcoFuture, a Web site dedicated to sustainability, has several suggestions on how to do this at www .ecofuture.org.)

- [ ] Instruct companies and organizations not to release your contact information for marketing, mailing, or promotional purposes.

- [ ] Avoid the post office's standard change of address (COA) form. If you must file a COA form, make it a temporary change that lasts less than a year so that the information doesn't end up in a permanent COA database to be released to others.

- [ ] Avoid club cards used by stores. They are used to track purchases and send promotional materials. Your name may also be sold to other marketers.

- [ ] Post a "no flyers" or "no junk mail" sign on your mailbox.

- [ ] If your paper clutter is beyond redemption, get help from a professional organizer.

- [ ] Remove your name from direct marketing lists.

7

Inheritances: Who Gets Grandfather's Clock?

"Our minds become clear and open in a home that is free from the chaos of possessions. This is not about throwing everything away; it is about keeping a sense of yourself and your life's journey."
—Jane Tidbury, author of *Zen Style*

"I put memories in a special chest of drawers," my friend Gordon wrote in a letter to me. "It is a rather fine piece, elm burl I think, although because of the deep rich graining and yellow glow, it might be willow. It sits on legs that appear fragile, like those of a small deer, but I know the body of the chest with its row on row of little drawers is strong and securely placed. That is a good thing—those legs that support all those drawers—for they hold everything that is precious to me. That drawer at the far right? It contains my grandfather's pocket watch on a chain with a five-dollar gold piece. Just below is the drawer with memories of the ranch where I spent my summers catching gophers. Another holds my mother's dangly earrings and with them, visions of her, not twisted and deformed and in pain but wearing a deep-red, strapless gown and elbow-length kid gloves . . . how stunning and gorgeous and magical she was. I move from drawer to drawer, opening and closing each one until finally I step back and see the chest, closed, contained, and restored. Then I take out the wax and give it a good shine."

Gordon's chest of drawers holds memories that enrich the fabric of his personal journey. They whisper words and conjure up images that anchor his life with a sense of belonging. Each object in that chest, wrapped in silken layers of love, has purpose and a special place in his life. Clutter? Hardly.

But it isn't always so. Inherited objects are curses as often as they are blessings. Inheriting money is straightforward. Extra cash can retire school loans, pay off the car, and cushion old age. But inheriting possessions is fraught with challenges for those who give and for those who get.

When we accept objects that don't serve a purpose or, unlike Gordon's treasures, do not enrich our sense of self, they devolve into clutter—and not just in our home. They can also clutter our heart and soul. According to feng shui philosophy, every object in our physical environment affects our peace of mind. We are wise to thoughtfully choose what we live with, and this includes gifts left to us by others. While we may have fond memories of whoop-ups around Grandma's dining table, unless we need a table, it is best left for others to enjoy.

Yet we might want to keep a tangible link to our loved ones. I felt this way about a dresser that had belonged to my grandmother. Its smooth, rounded lines made a novel focus in my otherwise conventional bedroom, but eventually my taste changed and I moved it into the attic. Later, my commitment to unclutter my home led me into the attic and back to the dresser. I wanted to preserve my grandmother's memory and this piece of my family's past, but the dresser had lost its usefulness long ago. No other family member wanted it. I had become its reluctant custodian.

After a bit of an internal struggle—was I diminishing or compromising Grandma's memory?—I decided to let it go and passed on the dresser to a young woman who proudly displays it as a gracious example of heritage furniture. By releasing it, I cleared a space in my home and gave Grandma's dresser a new purpose.

Turning objects once owned by loved ones into art is a distinctive way to capture the essence of a person while still conquering clutter. "My sister wanted a special remembrance of Mom," my friend Marianne told me. "Marlana—she's the creative one— gathered Mom's sewing thimbles, tiny delft wooden shoes that reflected her Dutch heritage, lace handkerchiefs, photographs, and other tokens of her life and arranged them in shadow boxes, one for each sibling. They speak of Mom in a very private, very personal way. The rest of her things went to charity."

Sadly, there are situations in which keepsakes infuse families with negative energy that can divide them. Wills and estate lawyer Brenda Milbrath cautions that all too frequently family treasures come bound in layers of potential dissention. "A family can appear entirely cohesive, but the true nature of the relationships and underlying family issues are bared when the last parent dies," she said. "The reason to play the good daughter or caring son role disappears." Ms. Milbrath related a case on which she spent several days with the family of deceased parents. "I was charged with mediating the entire contents of their home. The children would not agree on anything. If one person expressed an interest in an item, another wanted it. Spouses were behind the scene, vying for the grandfather clock or the good china." Like most clutter, this stuff created unbelievable havoc.

Even something as small as a Christmas tree ornament can ignite the fires of family destruction. Before her parents died, Carrie had expressed the desire for a particular decoration that held special meaning. Her mother gave Carrie the little glass ball and then willed her the entire collection of tree ornaments. When the woman died, another daughter, who also had an attachment to these ornaments, demanded that her sister share the collection. Sadly, their mother's death divided more than Christmas keepsakes.

It's unfortunate when the death of parents leads to family turmoil. "If everything is out in the open, there's far less potential for problems," said Ms. Milbrath. She strongly suggests that families discuss together the ultimate disposition of things while parents are living, for even a seemingly insignificant item can cause irreparable family divisions. Write the dispositions on paper and give each family member a copy. Label furniture and special items with the names of their future caretakers. Above all, ensure that any dissentions are resolved before death.

Feng shui experts agree that we must make these decisions with care. If an object is tarnished by bitterness or has no meaningful or useful purpose in our homes, then it is best left for others. In its place, we should select items that enhance life. Inherited items that are well loved give us a sense of continuity. Like the treasures in Gordon's chest, these are the remembrances that delight and inspire. They can weld the generations together in a bond of their unique history, for when inherited possessions are chosen with care and given with love, they are gifts worthy of the space we give them in our homes and in our hearts.

CLUTTER BUSTERS

☐ **Think carefully before taking inheritances that encumber your living space or might cause conflicts in the family.**

☐ **The object is not the person. Small mementos are just as comforting as Grandma's dresser.**

☐ **If family members cannot agree on the division of inheritances, consider putting the goods up for auction. Family members can bid along with others.**

☐ **Honor gifts you do not want by giving them to another family member or by donating them to museums, archives, or charity.**

☐ **Inheritance decisions have powerful consequences. Parents are wise to initiate a thoughtful discussion with all members present. Open discussions about family possessions can prevent future heartache and avoidable stress. Remember to write down all decisions.**

SECTION TWO
Mental Clutter

Expectations, distractions, and obligations
that affect our peace of mind.

C H A P T E R 8

The Time of Our Life

"Life is too short to stuff mushrooms."
—Shirley Conran, author

"I like the idea of the siesta. To my mind it is the perfect comple-
ment to the day. For me, an ideal schedule would be, up early in
the morning, have a bit of quiet time over morning coffee, then
blast into the day's activities. At around 2:30 PM—just cancel the
afternoon! Yep, just do away with it and replace it with a civilized
little afternoon nap. Now at about 4 PM you're up and ready to take
on the world again. Unfortunately, our society is not in sync with
this arrangement, so I guess I will just have to continue dragging
myself through those drowsy afternoon hours," Steve MacDowall
wrote in *The Thursday File*, his inspirational weekly e-newsletter.

What a sensible idea. Instead, weeks dissolve into a series of
Mondays as we shoehorn bits of life between too many demands.
As Prozac replaces poetry and chaos smothers serenity, we

wallow in a spiritually toxic brew. We've become time warriors. With "24/7" as our battle cry and armed with e-everything, we thrust and parry on a time-stressed, overworked battlefield. And by God, we're gonna win.

And then what? As my mother succinctly puts it, we die, of course.

Although this century has more labor-saving devices than all previous ages combined, we have even less time to plant, let alone smell, the roses. "Overwork is the decade's cocaine, the problem without a name," psychologist Bryan Robinson wrote in an article in *Fast Company*. Robinson adds that Americans now toil an average of forty-six hours per week (fifty-two hours, if you count take-home work), slipping past the Japanese as the longest-working citizens of any advanced industrial country. In a twist of irony, we play a dangerous roulette with our physical and mental health that sabotages the very results we seek to achieve.

We ought to go Dutch.

While these folks have the edge on wooden shoes and wind-mills, they also have government legislation that supports a less work-dominated culture. Many Dutch citizens enjoy an enviable work-life balance through a smorgasbord of choices, from three-day work weeks or compressed scheduling, to work weeks of between twenty-four and forty hours. Six weeks of vacation is the norm. Many in France and Germany also enjoy work weeks of forty hours or less with longer legislated vacation periods than most North Americans enjoy. Unlike many of their New World colleagues, the Europeans actually take their days off.

But when they do escape the daily grind, it's not all picnics and sandy beaches. According to a study by the Netherlands's

Tilburg University, some people are so keyed in to work that they suffer from leisure sickness. Headaches, migraines, colds, flus, and nausea plague them during their time off. Interestingly, the illnesses disappear when they return to work. The study concludes that leisure sickness stems not from a lack of general health but from a preoccupation with work, difficulty relaxing, and guilt for not being on the job.

Dr. Pauline Bellecci, an internal medicine specialist in Waycross, Georgia, commented, "We're hooked on the noise and motion that gives us the illusion of importance." She sees our leisure time shrinking "and along with it our health status as we are too busy to exercise, eat properly, or spend time with family or on creative pursuits."

Instead, we bolt into the office on a caffeine high, wolf down fast food, and, at the end of the day, collapse in front of the tube. All this, plus chronic sleep deprivation (47 percent of us sacrifice shut-eye to maintain our busy lives), fosters internal stress that, according to Stanford University neuroscientist Robert Sapolsky, affects the digestive system and contributes to heart disease. Strokes, once the bane of the elderly, now afflict thirty- and forty-year-olds. Internal stress can even suppress ovulation.

Yet even as our hurried society is killing us, we embrace it—fiercely. "We live in a culture of consumption," asserted University of Victoria professor Daniel Laskarin. "Many of us sacrifice more than half of our lives doing things we don't enjoy to buy things we don't need. We have plenty, yet feel dissatisfied." Prof. Laskarin believes that we purchase our participation in society—our sense of belonging. "We buy our cool. The only way out is to stop and ask what we really want instead of letting the media and big business tell us."

That's just what Sarah did. The once frazzled-to-the-bone office manager and single mom of two school-aged boys had a frantic life typical of do-it-all parents. "I rushed through the days in a frenzy that left me panting," she said. "It was like running a marathon, but without a finish line. The pace was killing me. Then I realized that the clutter in my life was everywhere. I wanted breathing room—living room."

It took the better part of a year, but Sarah delved into herself and surfaced with a clear vision of the life she wanted. "I'd lost all direction. I was living in a maze of endless routines and meaning-less activities."

Sarah uncluttered her life, one commitment at a time. "I pur-posely under-scheduled. At first, I felt guilty not always doing something. I was used to squeezing something into every ambu-latory hour. Now I divide the day into three sections [morning, afternoon, evening] and keep one free. Most days it works. And I don't do stuff just because everyone else does." Sarah avoided unnecessary meetings and committee work, simplified meals, and instituted potluck dinners for family get-togethers. "The boys help with the housework, and I give them a limit of two out-of-school activities, one that must be within walking distance of home. I'm not going to live in the car anymore."

Sarah wanted more out of life and less in it—and she got it. At the office, she now takes regular breaks instead of working through them. Sarah has recognized she isn't indispensable and uses her sick days when she needs them. "I think women, espe-cially mothers, feel guilty if they're not knocking themselves out for everyone else. I had to take back my life and my power. I feel such relief."

She admitted that it's a daily battle but the paybacks are priceless. Now instead of a quick wave as she passes her neighbors, she stops for a chat. "I've come to know them and discovered that I live among talented and generous people. I became reacquainted with my God and see and accept the many blessings around me—and I enjoy work more." Sarah said that her goal is to be fully present in everything she does. "I want to appreciate the challenges at work and see them as opportunities to learn. When I talk with my kids I want to really hear what they say and feel the good that surrounds me." Sarah admitted that life still has its crazy times. "Stuff comes at me all the time. But now when I have a decision to make, I consider how it will affect my schedule, my time with the kids, and—this is the big one—how it will affect me."

Uncluttering our time starts when we rise in the morning, the most delicious part of the day. Let the day unfold leisurely. Adjust your bedtime to get up an hour earlier to linger over coffee or take a stroll. Let the sound of birds be the first music of the day. The calm this creates seeps into the soul and stays with us even if the rest of the day jangles.

Plan tomorrow today. I've kept the habit of making an activity plan for the next day from my years of teaching school. This might include reminders to send a birthday card or to gas up the car. Other days it lists phone calls to return, a speech to research, and meetings to attend. Whatever is *on* the list is *off* my mind and I can enjoy my evening (and my sleep) without a flurry of to-dos floating around my head.

It's amazing what gets accomplished when we allow time to really focus (and finish) a task without fretting about what is next. If a term paper is due, give it your attention and put the social life on hold. Plan an extra fifteen minutes between appointments. Get an easy-care haircut. Dress simply. Give up nail polish. Most importantly, analyze *what* you do. If an activity enhances your life, embrace it and give it all the attention it deserves. If not, it's clutter and it's got to go.

Women, in particular, need off-duty time. I giggle when my buddies and I talk about this. We muse about turning off the phones to read a book or disappearing for a walk or just playing with the cat. We're always on duty, they tell me. "Even when I'm watching Angie's swim lesson, I'm making a grocery list or planning dinner," my neighbor said.

As author and activist Peace Pilgrim wrote in her wonderful book *Steps Towards Inner Peace*, life can be full but satisfying if we live with a clear purpose. "If [your life] is overcrowded, you are doing more than is right for you to do, more than is your job in the total scheme of things. There is a great freedom in simplicity of living," wrote this extraordinary woman who spread her message of peace and uncluttered living while walking throughout America—more than 25,000 miles—until her death in 1981 at age seventy-two.

While harnessing the activities that clutter time might not increase our net worth, it dramatically increases our life's worth. When we boot out the time thieves, we can rebalance life's pragmatism and poetry. By living purposefully, we can create a life of immense contentment.

C L U T T E R   B U S T E R S

- ☐ **Do it now. Procrastination paralyzes.**

- ☐ **Delegate tasks and involve partners and children.**

- ☐ **Schedule time each day just for yourself.**

- ☐ **Control electronics. Turn off telephone ringers and pagers at night. Turn off your cell phone during family or relationship time.**

- ☐ **Turn off the TV and take a walk.**

- ☐ **Plan time to eat well and get sufficient sleep.**

- ☐ **Cut back on caffeine.**

- ☐ **Sleep more. Studies show that many of us regularly complain that we're flat-out tired.**

- ☐ **Adopt an alternate form of commuting a few days each week. Try biking, walking, or taking the bus. This slows time down and builds in time for exercise and reflection.**

- ☐ **Work with passion. If your present job is unfulfilling, look for alternatives.**

□ Multitasking, whatever its advantages, fractures effectiveness and creates pressure. Screen out distractions and forgo multitasking to focus on just one task at a time.

□ Reclaim after-work hours by limiting committees, "business" socials, and high-maintenance acquaintances.

□ Resist the temptation to clutter the kids' schedules. (See chapter 13.)

Tune Out the Noise

"You don't have to be noisy to be effective."
—Source unknown

"Y'all hear that racket?" I heard a Texan tourist say to her partner as they walked along a Parisian boulevard. "Must be rush hour."

Noise—lots of noise—defines the City of Lights as surely as the pigeons that perch on its ancient rooftops. Each year ten million visitors flood Paris to revel in its glorious monuments, grand avenues, and trendy brasseries. It's magnificent—and exhausting. Like legions of Napoleonic bees, Paris bustles day and night. The crescendo begins in the morning when the first café awnings spread over sleepy sidewalks. Then the city's music bursts into a fanfare as cars and motorcycles swoosh down avenues, airplanes roar overhead, and yappy Parisian pooches—the bane of unwary pedestrians—take to the streets. As the evening wanes, the city's cacophony of trumpeting and blaring sounds soften until, in the early morning, it tunes up for the new day.

Except on Sunday mornings. That's when the nerve-jangling racket fades and Paris sings. And sing it did as I idled in a café near the Seine at daybreak listening to church bells. Leaves fluttered on branches as songbirds chirped. The boulevard seemed wider, the trees greener, the steel-blue sky softer as time slowed to an andante pace. In this short interlude, I heard the heart of Paris beat.

That morning in Paris still replays in my head. Until then, I was oblivious to the bustle, the clamor, and the continuous hum that underpins everyday life. It becomes part of audio wallpaper, an invisible yet dynamic backdrop some call "nuisance noise."

Experts define nuisance noise as unwanted sound. This noise clutter is, of course, a matter of taste. Some prefer Metallica to Mendelssohn. My passion for bagpipe jigs sends Bob for cover. But whining lawn mowers and weed-whackers, raucous neighbors, and the shrill of ringing cell phones creates soul-crashing upheaval in most of us. Like tossing about on rough seas, noise clutter can destroy our inner balance while cranking up the blood pressure. It grinds us down as surely as does the midday traffic on the Champs-Elysées.

My daughter, Carley, who moved from our peaceful little city on the West Coast to study in Montreal, offered her commentary on noise clutter. "It freaks me out. Here I am, doing the morning coffee thing, and the garbage truck starts banging and booming down the alley. Then there's the 3 AM scene when the bars close. It gets so rowdy that I actually notice when it's quiet. And," she said after a calculated pause, "it's distracting, especially when I'm studying." (That last comment is, naturally, a rhapsody to this mother's ears.)

While noise is transient and impermanent—and we may even resign ourselves to live with it—the effects of noise are not. Unrelenting racket is costing us millions. According to a *Los Angeles Times* article, European researchers from fifteen countries estimate that excessive noise results in an annual loss of 2 percent of their GNP.

And that's not all. New York City's audiological consultant, Maurice Miller, argues that prolonged exposure to noise causes one-third of the 33 million cases of significant hearing impairment in the United States. In Europe, where hearing loss is a leading occupational disease, 25 to 35 million people work in environments with potentially dangerous noise levels. According to a Sheffield University study, British cities are up to ten times noisier than they were a decade ago. Even the tranquility of the countryside is sideswiped as freeways and flight paths increase.

A report conducted by the *Houston Chronicle* also blew the whistle on environmental noise clutter. While not more than 40 to 50 decibels (dB) are recommended for physical and psychological well-being, gas-powered lawn mowers spit out 90 dB of noise in addition to harmful waste emissions. If we add lurching delivery trucks, car traffic, horns honking, car alarms, airline traffic, and the occasional police or ambulance siren, we have enough noise clutter to wear us down, and break our hearts.

Scientists in Germany are studying a link between stress-inducing noise and heart attacks. Audiologist Dr. Deepak Prasher, a leading expert on this issue, wrote that high volumes of traffic, especially at night, can trigger chronic stress, leading to ulcers and heart disease. And, despite our most ardent attempts to remain young, noise may cause enough stress to accelerate aging, induce depression, and increase anxiety. It also jinxes our hopes for sweet dreams. A study by the Environmental Protection Agency indicates that "intermittent and impulsive" noise is one of the chief culprits in disturbing sleep, making us moody, inattentive, and prone to accidents. And if stumbling into work blurry-eyed isn't enough, the bleeps and grinds of fax machines and photocopiers, ringing phones, and colleagues with stage-voice training might finish you off.

Noise also affects kids. Children living in noisy or chaotic circumstances experience increased anxiety as well as learning difficulties. Purdue University psychologist Theodore Wachs purports that students living by or attending schools near airports experience more trouble learning to read than those in quieter neighborhoods. A study by Don Campbell, author of *The Mozart Effect*, indicates that children attending a school located close to passing trains were eleven months behind those in calmer areas. So let's turn down the volume and give the kids a chance.

Is nuisance noise a *fait accompli*? I think not. As the volume in our world increases, so do attempts to fight back. Each spring, the League for the Hard of Hearing sponsors International Noise Awareness Day. Initially an effort to focus attention on noise levels in New York City, the event has spread to more than thirty countries. And it's creating change. Hong Kong's Office of Telecommunications is under pressure to end the use of cell phones in some public places (apparently libraries, movie theaters, and even churches are open territory) by installing jamming devices. Throughout North America, ambulance, fire, and police departments are reviewing their siren policies. Civilians also need to lower their volume. In one tragic circumstance, an ambulance on an emergency call crashed into a car, killing the driver. A witness said that the car stereo was so loud that the driver may not have heard the ambulance siren.

Vancouver's Right to Quiet Society has joined other sound-burned citizens across North America and Europe to demand that legislators outlaw gas-powered leaf blowers. Since 1982 the group has been educating communities and lobbying politicians for less noise. They maintain that a quiet environment is a basic human need, like clean air and water. With their efforts and those of groups elsewhere, these "quiet advocates" are exerting pressure to tone down their cities. In many places "quiet gardeners" who use only hand tools are gaining ground as they soundlessly cut and clip away.

More than forty cities in California have banned leaf blowers, and others across the continent are plotting the demise of these egregious noise bullies that rage at 110 dB. As Ted Reuter wrote in the *Christian Science Monitor*, "Leaf blowers are a perfect example of technology run amok. They blare and screech, kick up dirt and dust, and accomplish nothing." Former Los Angeles city councilor Marvin Braude contended that before gas leaf blowers were banned there, they emitted 18,000 tons of carcinogenic pollutants into the city air each year.

"Imagine hearing the wind speak," my husband said, recalling his time in the Arctic. "That's what real quiet is—when the slightest sound can travel forever." His comments reminded me of the lilting tinkle of bicycle bells on Sark, a Lilliputian island off the northern coast of France. No noise clutter there—just the sounds of a gentler way of life. All motor vehicles (save a handful of farming tractors) are banned. Heavy industry is likewise snubbed. Instead of traffic drone, the island resonates with the clonking of horses pulling wagons, islanders peddling bikes, and folks greeting each other as they meander along "The Avenue," Sark's main street.

While researching this tiny oasis for a story I was writing, I realized why two hours in the reverberating atmosphere of a city mall is fatiguing, while a full day strolling along Sark's cliff tops is energizing. "We choke space with continuous music, chatter. . . . It is simply there to fill the vacuum. When the noise stops there is no inner music to take its place," wrote Anne Morrow Lindberg in her timeless treasure, *Gift from the Sea*. Her words emphasize that time spent in a peaceful and spiritual setting allows the mind to find its own rhythm, not one dictated by external influences.

A new trend in home design includes a serenity chamber, a space dedicated to silence and meditation. There the soul thrives in the absence of noise. When we tune out noise, we open ourselves to the gentle loveliness of nature's music—and it is this music that energizes the soul and nurtures creativity.

Like selecting objects for our home, the sounds we live with should be useful, spiritually enhancing, or exceedingly beautiful. All the rest is clutter.

CLUTTER BUSTERS

Even in busy metropolitan areas, noise clutter can be mitigated. Take an inventory of the noises around you. Listen carefully to the sounds in your interior and exterior living spaces to determine those that annoy, distract, or increase anxiety.

☐ **Use area carpets and drapes. Hard surfaces magnify sound.**

☐ **In "open-concept" work stations, ask for sound-reducing cubicle paneling and carpeting. Locate office machinery and copy centers away from work areas.**

☐ **Double- or triple-pane windows reduce outside noise and the heat bill.**

☐ **Place rubber mats under noisy appliances.**

☐ **Turn off computers when not in use. They emit a low wheeze that contributes to "white noise."**

☐ **Turn off dimmer-switch lights when leaving a room. Like computers, they emit a low-level hum.**

☐ **Oil squeaky hinges.**

☐ **Give yourself a mini-mental vacation and turn off phone ringers during meals and when you are relaxing.**

☐ Think of your grandmother when you reach for electric appliances. Try the muscle-powered versions to eliminate noise and firm up those arm muscles as well. To avoid the rumble of the dishwasher and the clothes dryer, consider hand-washing dishes and air-drying laundry.

☐ Become a "quiet gardener." Use hand gardening tools and consider a push lawnmower. (You'll get a bit of exercise and endear yourself to the neighbors.) If you have a gardening service, choose one that uses quiet tools.

☐ Build a berm. Soil, trees, and plants are effective sound barriers.

☐ Consciously choose the sounds in your home and work environments. Consider mini-fountains or soft music over TV and radio for background sound.

☐ Speak up if you dislike the "second-hand" music that is piped into restaurants, offices, shops, and other public places.

☐ Help curb auto boom. In Copenhagen, 50 percent of workers walk or bike to work.

☐ Get organized. Many communities have action groups who lobby for restrictions on noise generators, such as gas-powered gardening tools, and times for garbage pickup and truck deliveries.

☐ Designate a room in your house as a sanctuary, even if it doubles as a guest room.

☐ Plan quiet times. Consider a silent retreat. See www.retreatsonline.com or search for monastery retreats.

10

Techno-Clutter

"...lead us not into temptation, but deliver us from e-mail."
—Source unknown

There I sat, waiting for the bus on a crisp autumn morning. All was calm as I scanned the newspaper, welcoming the gentle entrée to the day. Then in a swoosh of shrills the "cell folk" arrived. Some of them chattered nonstop into their Mars Bar look-alikes while others fingered Palm Pilots and checked their e-mail. A few feverishly tapped away on laptops. Like a tsunami, the morning calm dissipated in a wave of sonority.

While the blessings of technology are indisputable, it has the potential to overpower our lives. A gazillion Web hits answer the simplest question, e-mails seem to multiply like flies on roadkill, and with digital determination, cell phones barge into board-rooms, bars, and even bathrooms. Like Alice tumbling into the rabbit hole, we're dizzy with the possibilities of the latest, fastest, and coolest inventions—stuff I call techno-clutter.

We have become fractured, uptight, and stressed as communications become easier, cheaper, and quicker. More than eighteen billion e-messages float through cyberspace daily, each demanding an instant response that gobbles hours of time each week. Jokes from well-meaning friends, solicitations (both naughty and nice), and life-affirming instructions intended to soothe the spirit nestle among news from friends and work-related information, swamping our lives without mercy, and often, without invitation.

But let's admit it: technology dominates the zeitgeist. A survey of 2,000 respondents conducted by Priority Management Systems revealed that more than 100 million North Americans now use the Web. By 2006 this number will more than double. Cell phone use has also swelled. Hong Kong's 6.9 million people have more than 5.2 million cell phones. According to the International Telecommunications Union, nearly 50 percent of Americans own a cell phone and 7.5 million Americans use them exclusively.

Our fascination with technology slips our lives into fast-forward as we are seduced by its considerable advantages. Who can dispute the research advantages of the Internet, the cut-and-paste efficiency of word processing, or the affordable convenience of e-mail? Cell phones can be crucial in emergencies and voice mail protects important messages. Technology gives us the flexibility to work anywhere, anytime, and its educational possibilities are unheralded.

It also puts us in a state of continual "cognitive interruptus," said Priority Management Systems founder Daniel Stamp.

"Whether it's the phone, e-mail, or pager, every interruption diverts us from our task. We estimate that the average worker is distracted on average every eight minutes. As it takes two to three minutes to refocus, efficiency goes down as anxiety goes up."

I sympathized with Linda, who works in the public sector. "I spend at least a good hour each day reading and responding to e-mail. People want replies immediately; there's no time to be nice. Snippy and short—that's what they get. Life has become too intense. There's just too much of everything. It's crazy making."

A senior manager in the health-care field told me that she has a constant backlog of three hundred e-mails. "I'll never catch up."

And then there's spam, the barrage of unwanted and unsolicited messages that observers say comprises the bulk of all e-mail. Spamming is a booming industry. As with other clutter, it bogs us down, affecting productivity and our wallets as we sort through them: Internet service providers incur heavy expenses beefing up their networks to filter out spam. These costs are often passed on to consumers.

"We're suffering from digital depression," said Mr. Stamp. "Technology tethers us to the workplace wherever we are. There's no downtime, no escape, unless we take control. With clients around the world, I have to be connected. I've got all the latest technology, but I manage it." He told me that he puts an iron fence around the first hour and a half each day. "No one interrupts. What I accomplish during that time is often equivalent to what it might take eight hours to do otherwise."

Mr. Stamp's mastery over techno-terrorists may be the exception. In a recent survey, 39 percent of participants said that they use the phone in the bathroom.

The allure of the virtual world reaches far beyond the john. Just ask the kids. According to a recent Toronto-based survey, one-third of the 1,000 teenagers questioned engage in "telephony," a multitasking skill of flipping channels with the TV's remote control while messaging their friends on the Internet. They own more cell phones than Dad does fishing flies, and e-pals are more abundant than real ones. "Like, tech's happenin', man. It's cool," a with-it, wired-in adolescent told me.

It's going to get cooler. Concept cars with feelings unveiled at a recent Tokyo car show promise to frown, cry, and smile as well as take your pulse and measure your sweat. The Internet Fridge is on the drawing boards. With the flick of a computer chip and a videophone, this souped-up icebox will signal when the ketchup bottle is empty, summon a recipe for ginger marmalade, or download a video on how to Martha Stewart the Sunday roast. What's more, bathroom scales will measure more than weight; they'll transmit bio-specifics to your doctor. "Smart" mirrors will scroll the daily news headlines while you brush your teeth.

The choice between real advantages and perceived need determines our load of techno-clutter. As alluring as today's and future inventions are—and they are amazing—we need to determine if they really serve us. Are we so in need of being connected that we can't take a stroll without a beeper or cell phone? Do we want our kids living and learning vicariously, turning into a second-hand imagination generation? Is it possible to balance or completely sidestep the techno-craze and still function in this high-powered Age of Urgency?

Pamela Charlesworth, a much-in-demand architect and dynamic community volunteer, thinks it is. Although this Canadian-based professional has clients as far off as Germany, she resists "outside circuitry." She maintains an enviable Zen-like calm as she sails through days packed with on-site meetings, consultations with clients, sub-traders and property managers—all without a cell phone, pager, e-mail, or other basic tech-assistants. "I want to talk, negotiate, and suggest if need be," explained Mrs. Charlesworth. "I need to sense my client. I can't do that in an e-mail."

She cherry-picks the technology that works for her and rejects the rest. Although computer-generated design is in the fore, Mrs. Charlesworth artfully uses pencil, pen, and paper to produce her drawings. "I construct my designs with all of me—my head, my hands, my heart." She organizes her day with the aid of a flesh-and-blood assistant and a telephone. The fax machine is her one concession. "We've furnished entire homes—put sheets on the beds and cutlery in the drawers—via phone, fax, and courier," she said. "I don't need anything else. As for computers and the Internet? I want to connect eye-to-eye with those I work with, to learn from what they say and how they say it—to have the advantage of the serendipitous moment."

Mrs. Charlesworth's decision to shun new technology might appear eccentric, but her courage to choose what she needs and to select what enhances and empowers her inner processes celebrates personal choice. "Technology has a minimal place in my life. People first. That's just how it is," she said.

Former municipal councilor Cheryle Scott, who also rejects new technology, feels that it creates a culture of false importance. "If something is truly critical, the police will find me." Ms. Scott also faults technology for cluttering more than our lives. "Our landfills are bursting with discarded answering and fax machines, obsolete computers, and the like."

By nixing advanced technology these women have taken what might be seen as extreme positions. Is there a middle ground? I think there is. We can take an inventory of which devices truly make life easier. We can filter what comes in and decide when and to what we respond. We can instill in our children the satisfaction of searching for answers the old-fashioned way, and with it the pleasure of finding the unexpected. And we can take a step back (or perhaps it's a step forward) by using a diary instead of a Palm Pilot and writing a letter or phoning instead of e-mailing. Above all, we can set boundaries and make technology serve us, not the other way around.

C L U T T E R   B U S T E R S

☐ **To avoid spam, subscribe to Internet service providers that filter e-mail. You might also try registering with E-mail Preference Services Limited (www.emailpreferenceservice.com).**

☐ **If you decide to purchase a spam blocker software package, choose one that offers advanced technology. Some filters will reduce spam messages but may not eliminate all of them.**

☐ **Avoid purchasing products advertised in spam messages, even if the product seems legitimate. Don't reply to spam messages, click on links, or follow the "remove from this list" instructions. If you do, the spammer knows that your address is active.**

☐ **Daniel Stamp of Priority Management offers seven strategies for effective e-mail management:**

1. *Turn off the message alert or visual message.*

   You wouldn't let mail carriers empty a mailbag on your desk ten times a day and you certainly wouldn't let them ring a bell with each delivery. That's what happens if you read each e-mail when it arrives. Turn off the alert or visual message and take control of your e-mail and your time.

2. *Treat e-mail like regular mail.*

   Try to check your e-mail at regular times in the day (i.e., early morning, midday, and late afternoon). Even if you receive a high volume of e-mails, you shouldn't check your e-mail more than four times a day. Throw out the junk or respond immediately to those that require your attention.

3. **Create short answers.**

   Short answers reduce the length and frequency of messages you receive. It's acceptable to send back a message that simply reads "Done" or "Thanks."

4. **Delete diligently.**

   Most people save too many e-mails. Delete messages as soon as you have responded to them. If you have to save something, transfer it to a folder.

5. **Use an auto-reply.**

   Use an auto-reply that tells people when you are out of the office. People may assume you've received and read urgent messages when in fact you're not even in the office

6. **Take control of your in-box.**

   Subscribe to e-mail services selectively. Get a separate e-mail address for personal communication or one that you give just to key contacts, just as you would an unlisted phone number.

7. **Use caution.**

   Sometimes it's too easy to hit the "Send" button and before you know it, you've sent words you will regret. In the end, it will take more time to do damage control than to let your emotions cool down before sending a message. Sarcasm or other attempts at humor can be misinterpreted. Remember that any e-mail you send could be forwarded and your message could go public.

Work: Tyranny or Transcendence?

"Our jobs are not our lives ...
just our current gig. We do have choices."
—Joshua Halberstam, author of
Work: *Making a Living and Making a Life*

"It was 1973 and I was almost fifty," Hilary Stewart said. The prolific author, illustrator, and expert on West Coast native culture was telling me why she quit her job as a TV set designer nearly thirty years ago. "I'd walk around the studio with a bulging file under my arm marked IMWAB [I Am Writing a Book]. Whenever I could, I'd head into my office, close the door, and work away on it. Eventually I had to make a choice, so I saved my money and when I felt ready, I made the leap. It was a bit of a struggle to make ends meet so I cut expenses to the bone, even gathered windfall apples and went without cream in my coffee. But I was determined."

And Hilary Stewart didn't just survive; she thrived! Her work is her joy. It flows through her life as naturally as the tides brushing the beaches of her Quadra Island home. Her resolve to test the Gods of Security and Pension Plans led to a profoundly meaningful life. Ms. Stewart finished that book and several others followed.

Meaningful work matters. At its most basic level, work satisfies our economic imperatives and signals our position in society. Through it, we pay the rent, buy groceries, and prepare for the future. But our work can also express who we are and provide reasons for getting on with life. Whether we wait tables at the local diner or manage a Wall Street brokerage house, meaningful work will showcase our special talents and foster deep satisfaction.

But unfulfilling work poisons our zest for living. It pilfers the blessings we deserve and can sour our heart and soul—and it can smother life with emotional and physical exhaustion. It clutters life with anxiety, boredom, resentments, and low self-esteem that can leave us bitter, wishing we were somewhere else or—caught in a vicious cycle of envy—someone else. Like all clutter, unfulfilling work clouds life with undercurrents of chaos that bite the heels of personal power.

Lack of recognition, gossipy workplaces, unhealthy physical environments, jobs without potential, and bosses without compassion all contribute to workplace clutter. And unhappiness at work is pervasive. Only 13 percent of men and 22 percent of women of the 10,000 surveyed for a British study declared that they were completely satisfied with their jobs. Another survey by the online version of Red magazine found that six out of ten women workers wished that they could quit their jobs.

Yet most of them won't. The lure of the next vacation, the annual raise, and the promise of a retirement pension keep many chained to the millstone. So does responsibility to family and insistent creditors. Doing what you really want might work for the folks with a healthy trust account, but what about the nine-to-fiver with real commitments and obligations?

Esperanza, my wonderful no-nonsense hairdresser, says it's all about attitude. Esperanza embodies the Quaker saying "Work is love made visible." The vase of flowers (a weekly gift from her husband) that dominates her studio pales next to her intoxicating zeal for life. Spirited Latin music floats through the air as she clips, curls, and tangos. A salve of genuine caring flows from the tip of her hairdresser's scissors toward the women who come for spiffy new looks. They leave with lighter hearts and heads ringing with Esperanza's kitchen-table wisdom.

"If you want to change jobs but can't, change your outlook," said this vivacious woman whose bosomy embraces could squeeze a yelp from Hulk Hogan. "I'm happy with what I do now, but like most of us, I've had jobs I detested. But hey, honey, we all have to work at something. Sometimes we just have to put on a good face and do our best to make the sun shine—especially when it's cloudy. And you know what?" she added with a broad, radiant smile. "When we look for the good in things in life, we find them, even in jobs we don't like."

While a positive outlook will bash the heck out of mental clutter, so will a dash of creativity. "For me, teaching subjects I don't like is workplace clutter," said Barbara, a teacher with a passion for history and a dislike for sports. "I adore history but have absolutely no talent when it comes to physical education. Fortunately, I have a colleague who agreed to trade my P.E. class for her history class. With one less subject to prepare, we both have more time to do what we're best at. Everyone wins, especially the kids."

A two-hour drive to work cluttered the job for Sue, a Vancouver-based senior account executive. "Driving in this city is horrendous. I'm an animal by the time I reach the office." Fortunately, Sue's company allowed her to work from home two days a week. "It's a good deal for them. I have fewer interruptions here than at the office so I'm actually more productive. And I save all that commuting time."

But what if we despise our work, can't stand the boss, dread Mondays, and die a little each time we punch the clock? If we look, there are often new opportunities within the same field. An operating-room nurse seeking relief from a highly charged atmosphere might retrain as a public health practitioner. A banker frustrated by the inflexibility of a large institution could set up his own financial counseling company. A divorce lawyer wearied of the thrust and parry of the courtroom might use her negotiating and problem-solving skills to teach mediation.

James, a marketing representative, handled his situation with patience and a plan. "I lived the life of a beer commercial," he said of his job. "I sat in the VIP boxes at the games, skied, golfed, and fished at the best places." By the time gray hairs highlighted the boyish blond curls and his growing family clamored for attention, the company ladder was cleared for his assent. All he had to do was scoot up the rungs. That's when James quit.

"I wanted to see my boys grow up. Although the company never came out and said it, it expected us to live the job," he explained. "Sure, [the bosses] said it's important to balance our lives, even offered us courses on how to do it, but all the guys knew that quarterly objectives came first. The money and all that, well, it was nice, but they owned me—and my time."

James knew his skills had value but said that he "didn't want to take huge risks, so I started keeping an eye out for something related to my industry." He talked with people, asked what was happening in their companies, and watched how they were treated. Then he started dropping comments to likely employers, letting them know that he might be looking around. Within a year, James had another position with a company where people actually take their vacations. "The money's great, I love the challenge—and I have time with my boys."

I asked James what advice he'll give his sons when they step into the workforce. Will he encourage passion or pension? "I know it sounds clichéd, but I'll tell them to follow their hearts, not to be caught in golden handcuffs or seduced by power, not to let the job control their lives. If they can see that that's all clutter, the rest is easy."

Yet even as the balance between work and family tilts dangerously toward work, some companies recognize that a work-life balance is a priority in attracting and keeping staff. And when they do, studies indicate that sick days drop and productivity increases by almost 20 percent.

"I had just left a difficult relationship when I started working here," said Carol, a grocery store cashier. "My boss knew this when he hired me. I was emotionally fragile, but he took me on anyway, helped me through the bad days, and gave me time off when I needed it. Even though I could earn more working elsewhere,

I won't leave. The atmosphere is so positive. Working here is my therapy. Everyone smiles."

Donna, a former bank employee, took a huge risk when she left her job (with its enticements of security and benefits) to start a business offering tours of her city's walking trails and outdoor heritage. "Working at the bank suffocated me," she explained. Fully aware of the financial pitfalls of a seasonally based business, Donna did her homework first. She developed a solid business plan with a market survey, cultivated relationships with the tourist board, offered visiting journalists familiarization tours, and set up a strategic promotion program.

When we last spoke, she was madly planning the coming season after a promising first summer. "Sure there were risks and challenges in leaving my job, but life is full of those. I feel so alive now." For this resolute young woman, the decision to do what she loved rather than "go through the motions" defined her approach to life and made her intensely happy. "I believe we have a right to do what we love, but we have to be willing to invest in ourselves, plan carefully, learn what we need to know, focus our goals, and will ourselves to succeed."

Frances Litman, who was also locked into a job that had lost its shine, juggled two jobs before she turned a passion into a paycheck. The former editorial assistant discovered a natural chemistry with the camera after taking a photography course. "I fell in love with the camera. I studied and I practiced. Deep down I knew that photography was my calling, but could I make a living taking pictures? That was the challenge." Ms. Litman talked of beating back niggling thoughts like "working in the creative arts means living poor" and "taking pictures is not a 'real' job." I asked how she had made the switch from a union-protected job to an at-your-own-risk vocation. "It was a calculated risk," she responded thoughtfully. "I developed my photography business while still slugging it out at the newspaper. For three years, I essentially worked two jobs. Then I went for it. Now I can't imagine doing anything else." Like Hilary Stewart, whose books have never been out of print, Frances Litman is at the top of her game, consistently winning international honors and relishing every minute of it.

There are numerous examples of others who left unsatisfying work to find jobs that fulfill deeper needs and express personal values. A private detective entered the priesthood, a day-care worker is now a police constable, a former government bureaucrat creates magic as a film producer, and a former truck driver is now a successful sculptor.

"In most cases, those making a change have to confront what is important to them, to assess their values and deal with the ever-present social pressure of equating who we are with what we do," said employment counselor Hannah Green. "People often rate their self-worth according to the work they do."

The late Joseph Campbell, philosopher, mythologist, author, and teacher who popularized the phrase "follow your bliss," said that when we do this, doors we didn't even know existed will open. No doubt there's a good bit of testing along the way, but Campbell emphasized that when potential is fertilized with the power of directed passion, it blossoms to liberate our soul. It's how we create our heaven on earth and release genius.

The gripping melodies of a Mahler symphony, medical breakthroughs that cure polio and smallpox, at-home businesses that improve services for seniors, guided explorations in the country-side, moments captured in Litman photographs, and a page from Hilary Stewart's book all stem from working from the heart. Just as potent are heavenly handmade blintzes at the tiny shop down the street, crafts that fill neighborhood stores, and volunteers who share their talents. When work is "love made visible," it clobbers boredom, apathy, and ennui—the clutter of unfulfilling work. When work becomes an expression of our humanness, when it reveals who we are, when it resonates with passion and our deeper self, all things are possible. As the indomitable publisher Katherine Graham said, to love what you do and feel it matters—could anything be more fun?

C L U T T E R   B U S T E R S

☐ Think of work as a vehicle to express your values and who you are.

☐ Choose a job that showcases your talents.

☐ Use your creativity to make your work meaningful and to express your inner needs.

☐ Keep a positive attitude. Adjust your expectations.

☐ Doing what you love breeds success and builds confidence.

☐ Balance life by looking for flexible and creative approaches to work.

☐ Analyze your employer's philosophy on work-life balance. Consider flextime, job sharing, telecommuting, or part-time work.

☐ Refuse to take part in office gossip and other negative workplace activities.

☐ Listen for the call to follow your bliss. It is the source of your genius.

☐ If you decide to change your job, learn new skills and make contacts in your new field first.

☐ Consider transforming a hobby into paying work.

TV: Prime-time Clutter

"I find television very educating. Every time somebody turns on the set, I go into the other room and read a book."

—Groucho Marx, actor

I'm not sure who the Sopranos are.

I'm out of touch and out of tune. Several years ago, my family gave up watching television. We agreed that TV emitted more than low-grade radiation; it sucked away precious time, cluttered the house with constant babble, and muscled in on our relationships. My son, David, glued himself to the tube most evenings and I resented the inevitable clash when our program choices conflicted. Bob booed and cheered his way through the seasons watching big men kick balls through goal posts, toss them into hoops, and bat them out to left field.

While we didn't clock the national average of four hours of TV each day, nor were we among the 40 percent of families who eat dinner in front of the tube, time seemed to evaporate into the air-waves. After a voluntary reduction to one program a day failed (within days we were back to our normal pattern), we bit the bullet and pulled the plug.

As that first TV-free week began, remorse set in and nagging questions surfaced. Would David become a pop-culture outcast? What would Bob and I do on those dreary winter nights made bearable by real-buttered popcorn and Discovery Channel specials? What if *Globe & Mail* columnist John Barber was right when he said, "TV is the last touchstone of belonging"? When conversations turned to rehashing last night's episode of the latest hot show, would I be out of touch, like a hermit in a yurt? Would David, a typical teenager who still chuckled over Saturday morning cartoons, pressure us to "get with the program"?

Fortunately, it was a brief period of adjustment, but only because it was spring and the back garden beckoned. Forgotten flowerbeds emerged from tangled weeds. Bob pruned unruly blackberry canes as I planted vegetables. Together we nursed an herb garden. In place of TV news, we opted for newspapers and magazines. The radio provided the local and global view on current events.

Prime time became *our* time.

Of course, it wasn't all daffodils. David, in predictable teenage style, replaced TV drone with rap, techno-rave, and other equally irritating music. Bob missed the gridiron grind, and I wondered if Larry King still wore suspenders.

Spring stretched into summer. We were half a year into television abstinence. Gone were hard-selling commercials, parades of impossibly thin (and surgically improved) women, and life set to laughter tracks. As we *did* life instead of *watch* it, our days resonated with a gentler, clearer, quieter rhythm.

I became reacquainted with the nuances of the senses: the cadence of falling rain against the windows, the heady fragrances of my garden, and the velvety caress of early morning mist. Bob and I started biking more and driving less. There were fewer undone chores to nag David about. Days now ended without a trace of TV fatigue. Instead of putting up our feet and channel surfing, we'd take long after-dinner walks, or I'd feed my passion for British mystery novels. Freed from the seduction of late night miniseries, we got more sleep. Television simply faded from our lives.

But like someone drawn by the pull of an old addiction, I occasionally crave a TV fix. In an article for the *New York Times*, writer Frank Rich argued that television networks are "the single most constant power in the American cultural life since World War II." I agree. I'll admit that there are times when I want to numb out a demanding day in front of a light comedy. And of course I'm curious about what they'll be wearing when the Oscars roll around in March.

This raises the question: do I cheat? Catch a program or two on the sly? Get friends to videotape the odd show? You betcha. Like forbidden fruit, TV now holds a certain mystique. When I'm traveling, I check out the hotel room set, and Bob and I occasionally put a movie in the VCR.

Sometimes I still miss watching the news when a big story breaks or being in-the-know about the latest sitcom. Then I recall zoning out in front of programs I couldn't remember the next day and tussling with David over which program to watch or when to serve dinner. Besides, the space in my life that TV once occupied is gone. Bob and I wouldn't sacrifice our dinner-table chats (that often last until bedtime) for even one hour of reality TV.

While giving up the tube is not for everyone, seven million North Americans nixed the switch in April 2003 during TV Turnoff Week, an annual initiative sponsored by the TV-Turnoff Network, a nonprofit group dedicated to TV-free living. Of those participants, 17,000 people were first-timers. Second-grade student Drew Henderson of Donora, Pennsylvania, is quoted on the group's Web site as saying she really didn't like TV-Turnoff Week, "except I did notice that my grades went up and I was in a good mood all week."

For our family, pulling the plug eliminated one of our most potent and insidious sources of mental clutter. Gone is the banal hum of nuisance commercials, gunfights, and car crashes. And gone is the pressure to live in thirty-minute time slots. Now time expands, gently. Our home is a quiet, calm refuge, and the money we save on TV service is a welcome bonus.

Like clearing the clutter from an overstuffed closet, our lives have more space—acres of it. Instead of watching life, we ramble among the treasures in the backyard of our community, doing real things with real people. Unplugging the television plugged us in to a more authentic life. It's so good that we won't change a thing.

Thoughts to Ponder
(Courtesy of TV-Turnoff Network (www.tvturnoff.org))

☐ TV-free families average one hour of meaningful conversation per day as opposed to the national average of thirty-eight minutes per week.

□ TV-free families represent all occupations, income brackets, and levels of education.

□ Ninety-two percent of TV-free parents say that their children "never or rarely" complain about lack of TV, nor do they pressure parents to buy brand names and popular toys.

□ Eighty percent of TV-free people say that their relationships are stronger (more cuddle time).

□ The computer does not take the place of television, although 98 percent of TV-free families own one.

□ More than half of TV-free kids get all As in school.

□ The easiest way to combat decreased activity is to turn off the TV. Eleven percent of six- to seventeen-year-olds are significantly overweight, more than twice the number in the 1960s.

CLUTTER BUSTERS

☐ Brainstorm a wish list of activities that you would do if you had more time. Include the activities you liked doing as a kid.

☐ Keep a record of every program you watch for a couple of weeks and add up the time you spent with the tube. Take another look at the wish list; you just might be able to make some of them come true.

☐ Go for it and turn off the TV, but be flexible. If you simply can't miss a program, ask a friend to tape it.

☐ Turn on the radio and peruse the newspapers to keep current.

☐ After four weeks, celebrate. I'll bet you're so busy that you wonder how you had ever found time for *The Sopranos*.

Cluttered Kids

"Move over, sun, and give me some sky.
I've got me some wings and I'm ready to fly."
—American Spiritual

A Canadian newspaper reported that Upper Canada College, a 174-year-old private school in Toronto, has initiated the country's most expensive senior kindergarten program. At $19,000 per year (excluding registration fees, uniforms, etc.) the school promised to "educate every boy to reach his highest level of social, emotional, intellectual, artistic, and physical development." With this school producing many of the country's top politicians and professionals, admission to UCC is the first step toward what might be a glorious career. And for every one of the eighteen spaces available, three children are on the waiting list.

Dr. Rene van de Carr, an obstetrician in Hayward, California, has established a prenatal university. Her programs instruct parents on how to use music to stimulate their babies even before birth. Some experts agree that this and other practices van de Carr uses will advance the unborn child's intellectual and physical abilities. Others are skeptical.

But the message is clear: We want Super Kids. In an increasingly aggressive society, parents respond with the fear that their kids will be left behind. Spaces in good universities and vocational colleges are limited, and a solid education usually means a good job and with it a better chance for a fulfilling life. This begins with music lessons and math tutoring for preschoolers in hopes of snagging scholarships out from under the kid down the block. And we're willing to pay through the nose, bleed through every pore, and devote each waking hour to give our kids the edge.

But all we're getting is Cluttered Kids. These kids are over-organized. Even while they are still spitting up their food and messing up their diapers, their parents are training them for greatness. Before they can see over the kitchen counter, our Wunderkinder can surf the Net and connect with chat-mates in Japan or Uruguay. Instead of tunneling their way to China in the backyard, these tiny tykes are conducting interactive, multimedia explorations of simulated archeology digs—all without dirtying their Baby Gaps.

Psychologist Bonnie Leadbeater agrees with other child development experts that children today are over-scheduled, yet she conceded, "While a barrage of activities can tire out and drag kids down, it does give them opportunities to find their talents." Some of these hothouse kids will thrive, while others will bend under today's escalating expectations. Others, tragically, will break. Eating disorders, aggressive behavior, lying, cheating, and stealing are signals that kids are overly stressed. Studies show that one in twenty children under the age of ten exhibits signs of depression. In her book *Kidstress*, Georgia Witkin pointed out that bedwetting, insomnia, frequent colds, and the worsening of existing chronic ailments such as asthma, allergies, and even rheumatoid arthritis plague our children. She also emphasizes that suicides are the third leading cause of teenage deaths. Drug and alcohol abuse are on the rise and cigarette smoking is now a pediatric concern. Dr. David Elkind, professor of Child Study at Tufts University and author of *The Hurried Child*, wrote that in the United States, 10,000 young people die in substance abuse-related car accidents each year and two million teenagers are now alcoholics. Certainly not all of these calamities result from pressurized lifestyles, but Drs. Witkin and Elkind argue that they play a significant role.

Is there a solution, a middle way that ensures the best possible future for our children without losing them in a maze of compacted schedules and micromanaged lives? Use common sense, my mother would say.

Whatever a child's potential, they simply cannot do it all—at least not all at the same time. Uncluttering children's lives means encouraging activities that are fun and that develop talents, discipline, and character. It means culling activities that don't affirm who they are or don't give them a sense of joy or fulfillment. It means making choices that balance study, play, and family time.

But it's not easy for parents to allow their child's special gifts (and the privileges that come with achievement) go undeveloped, especially if they can give their child opportunities they didn't have. I know about this firsthand. At nine years old, my daughter,

Carley, was a promising judo student who won a major championship in her first competition. She loved the sport. Her coach, sensing a potential star, fast-tracked her into a competitive program. By twelve, she was training with no-nonsense coaches who prepared athletes for international matches. While she formerly had gentle encouragement, these trainers whacked the kids with bamboo sticks when they erred. Carley stopped smiling, and the fun and the joy of the sport dissolved into a mix of stress and anxiety. The emphasis on winning overshadowed all.

Before long, she'd had enough and she quit. But all was not lost. Although my daughter never stepped onto a Gold Medal podium, the skills she learned and the confidence she developed left a valuable legacy. Today this size-five bit-of-a-thing can still toss a hulking he-man over her shoulder, and she'll walk down any street she chooses.

Uncluttering childhood means more than just ditching daunting schedules. Kids need balance, space of their own—both physically and mentally—and a feeling that they are important to their parents and to society. Just as necessary are quality friendships and unorganized downtime to wander in the exclusive, magical world of childhood. While relentlessly practicing the tuba might someday wedge a crack in the doors of Julliard (and this is a wonderful thing), building fantasy forts from salvaged scraps, making paper dolls, and playing dress-up are just as important for a well-balanced childhood.

There's nothing like old-fashioned, kid-generated fun to unclutter childhood and learn life skills. During the summers when I was growing up, while moms and dads did mom-and-dad things, we played pickup baseball at the park, skipped rope, and terrorized the neighborhood with games of hide-and-seek. My friends and I amused ourselves dissecting bugs and dead birds we found during forays in the neighborhood (and later conducted some rather macabre funerals), not realizing until much later how much biology we were learning. We discovered how to get along with each other, made decisions on our own, and developed a few grass-roots marketing skills when we planned and promoted circuses we held in my best friend's garage.

Childhood back then was wrapped in the gift of time—uncluttered time, time to be creative, to wonder, and, during long summer vacation days, time to do nothing at all. Our mothers didn't arrange playdates for us; we'd just walk over to a buddy's place and knock on the door to ask if she could come out and play.

While my parents kept an eye on us, they didn't clutter us with overconcern. Sure, they gave us lessons if we wanted them, but they kept out of the way to let us make mistakes and learn from them, especially at school. Today's emphasis on parent-school involvement is admirable, but the need for children to achieve makes me question if it is parents or their progeny who derive the greatest benefit from homework assignments. When I first worked as a school teacher, I was amazed at the sophisticated projects some of my students produced. Reconstructions of Chinese communes complete with working wells, research papers with cutting-edge sources, and masterful art projects worthy of a Guggenheim exhibition attested to truly brilliant fifth graders— or perhaps overly involved parents. I soon declared that all major projects be done in class, by the kids.

Uncluttered kids have parents who step aside to let them be kids. These parents know that life is remembered in moments.

They give their children space to live one adventure at a time. Parents of uncluttered kids model balanced lives free from bustling schedules. They examine what their own actions say about their priorities and values. They encourage their children to discover their potential and not to fulfill a parent's missed opportunities. And they know that under nose rings and purple nail polish are great kids with promise who will blossom in their own time, in their own way.

Parents of uncluttered children relax and let their kids stretch into their days instead of packing them with commitments. They back off to let their kids stare out the window and explore, invent, and experiment. They let them learn by doing, failing, and succeeding. They teach their kids to embrace joy, face sorrow, make friends, and handle disappointments. They know that decency, compassion, and honesty in both personal and business relationships come first in life. And they know that supporting their children to do their best develops character, that priceless quality that is attained through hands-on life experiences.

These parents believe that scoring the perfect goal or achieving straight As should be celebrated, but they also know that peeling potatoes for a family dinner matters, too.

And who knows? When their children become parents and Saturdays roll around, they're likely to unclutter their own schedules and help their little ones dig to China or build fantasy forts, just for the fun of it.

C L U T T E R   B U S T E R S

☐ Unclutter your child's life by balancing school, time for friends and family, and organized activities.

☐ View children's activities as opportunities to discover their talents, make friends, and have fun, not as a stepping-stone to million-dollar contracts or national prominence.

☐ Educators agree that children develop physically and intellectually at their own rates and in their own time. Relax and let your children become their best selves, something they will do naturally if given space, love, and gentle guidance.

☐ Childhood is the time to explore. Provide a variety of activities for your children to choose from. Let them sift and sort and make changes.

☐ Encourage time each day for unorganized play.

☐ Children live in the present. Slow down. Let them enjoy it.

☐ Children learn about life by watching those around them. Model a balanced life that values the physical, emotional, and spiritual needs of the family and expresses the ethics, values, and morals you hope to see in your children as they mature.

☐ Encourage your children to fulfill their dreams—not yours.

14

Uncluttering the Holidays

"Christmas, children, is not a date. It's a state of mind."
—Mary Ellen Chase, writer and educator

You can't beat a cool margarita on a hot day, especially at Christmas.

Bob and I were far from home, sunning ourselves on a Mexican beach, desperately trying to feel guilty. It seemed the decent thing to do, given the season, but instead of being homesick, we felt as content as the pelicans fishing near us—and just a little smug, for we had exchanged the unforgiving Canadian winter and the pandemonium of the Christmas season for a low-key winter vacation in the sun. Our laid-back enclave was brimming with other turncoats who shared our goal: a saner, less chaotic, less expensive, and less cluttered holiday.

Some folks anticipate the season and make a ritual of shopping for gifts, addressing cards, baking special sweets, and planning sumptuous meals. "It's my favorite time of the year. Everything about it is magical," said Jane, who arrived at a neighborhood get-together with a wreath of stars twinkling in her hair. "When we were kids, Mom made Christmas so special. We'd hand-make decorations a couple of months ahead. Then we'd bake scads of cookies. As there wasn't much money to buy gifts, we made them. They were small things, but each was special, personal. Christmas was a delicious, wonderful time. And it still is."

For some, holiday celebrations are not as wonderful. In a survey conducted by Dateline NBC and *Prevention* magazine, 41 percent of respondents said that they find Christmas and Hanukkah as stressful as asking the boss for a raise. With so many details to manage and decisions to make (should we send cards to just the out-of-towners this year?), many of us resent the season long before it arrives.

Although we promote the holidays as a time for special people and joyful get-togethers, for many, it is cluttered with expectations, old hurts, obligations, and too many commitments packed into too few days. Time compresses as we juggle work and family expectations. And then there are the endless line-ups of last-minute shoppers, drop-by guests, week-long visitors, baking, cleaning, and squeezing one more party into a burgeoning social calendar.

There's often a deep divide between how we want things to be and how they really are. While we try to "make happy," old ghosts come out to play. Family conflicts, Uncle Hank's affair with the bottle, divorce, remarriage, co-parenting arrangements, illness, death, and religious differences can cloud the season with resentments, sadness, guilt, and anger.

"Emotions run high as familiar patterns of interaction occur in the context of gift-exchanges, religious worship, or the eventual settling in for a family meal," Herbert Rappaport wrote in *Holiday Blues*. With more than 36 percent of marriages ending in divorce (one-third involving children), Christmas isn't what it used to be. Parents want the best for their kids, but the strain of the season frazzles mix-and-match families trying to manage the seasonal hype, everyday demands, and the logistics of sharing the kids with the ex-spouse. Children often feel the tug of loyalties even if divorced parents celebrate the day *en famille*. All feel the artifice, even in the glow of gifts and good cheer. "I just want it to go away," said a divorced mother of two. "The happy family laughing around the Christmas tree is a cruel joke for people like me."

The holiday season also heightens the sense of loss for family and friends who live or work far from home. "We miss the connections with family and people we grew up with," said Mary Gavan, an immigrant from Cork, Ireland, and a nurse specializing in grief recovery. "Grief is a reaction to any change, be it moving to a new place or the death of loved ones, and Christmas is a time of extremes. It's a time that demands 'we will be jolly,' even if that's not how we feel." Ms. Gavan said it helps to plan a ritual that acknowledges the loss, such as a gathering of other orphaned folk or a visit to a gravesite. "We need to tell our story, to have someone acknowledge our feelings."

As Christmas bells ring, so do the cash registers. Even while we yearn to feel in harmony with the heavens, the sacred is often sacrificed on the altar of consumption. We deplete our bank accounts and max out the credit cards to ensure a perfect holiday season. The line blurs between our business and personal lives as party clothes for office celebrations, single malt scotch for the boss, and gifts for clients, potential clients, teachers, letter carriers, and others in our sphere of influence compete for cash.

But we can scale down the gift giving. A friend who shares my interest in out-of-print books routinely delights me with volumes she stumbles upon at flea markets. Others I know give completely clutterless gifts. Marianne's hefty loaf of homemade bread packed with nuts, grains, and all things wonderful, Paddy's hot toddy mix, and Julie's lavender and gooseberry jellies are one-of-a-kind-perfect—as are an invitation to see an afternoon movie, a bundle of homegrown herbs arranged with affection and presented with a hug, and coupons for house-sitting, dog-walking, or grass-cutting services.

While we can unclutter the holidays with thoughtful gift giving, we can also simply do less. Sarah Blake wrote in the *English Home* magazine, "The truth is, the only pressures of the season we feel are the ones we place on ourselves. Don't conform if you don't want to—Christmas is a time for pleasure and indulgence. If that means running away with a suitcase full of books to a quiet cottage with no telephone, then do it."

My friend Marianne and her husband, David, do just this, but instead of a cottage, they steal away on *Starkindred*, their trusty sailboat, for a weeklong escape among the islands near their home. "We have Christmas Eve dinner with the family and then off we go. It's the most relaxing time of the year for us," Marianne said.

Steve and Julie, who live thousands of miles apart from family, take clutter out of the holidays by making it a time just for them. "Last Christmas I finally felt connected to Vancouver— something my restless soul was unable to achieve since moving here twenty-odd years ago," Julie wrote in a post-season letter to me. "Although Steve and I remain nostalgic for family and the festive, food-laden Christmases we grew up with, we have finally found our peace and contentment in our new, more personal celebration. It had to do with creating and adopting new traditions. This year, we sidestepped the whirl around us to indulge in windy walks on the seawall where boats, large and small, bobbed with masts strung with every color of lights. We shopped for our unfussy Christmas dinner in the market by the harbor (our bird this year was grilled fresh duck, the skin crisped to mahogany brown and drizzled with peppercorn sauce). We listened to Ella Fitzgerald and just kicked back to let the bustle pass on by."

Uncluttering the holiday season is like sorting through a box of old photographs. We need to take a ruthless inventory, keep the best, and let go of the rest. It's a time to reflect and move forward—a time to bask in the warmth of old friendships and nurture new ones. And it's a time for renewal of the self, inside and out. If the spirit moves us (and the pocketbook doesn't protest), we can occasionally forget about the whole thing and skip town.

Like the first plunge off the high diving board, uncluttering the holidays takes a little chutzpah, but the subsequent leaps are pure joy. By making the holiday ours, we experience a season that resonates with our personal truth, one that turns down the volume of life a notch to give us mental and physical space to contemplate life's blessings. As Herbert Rappaport wrote, "Celebration provides us with the opportunity to underscore what we hold sacred. . . . Each of us has the capacity to shape and control the vibrancy of our celebrations and our lives."

Those who understand and love us will be happy we do.

CLUTTER BUSTERS

☐ **Make the season a celebration that reflects your needs and values.**

☐ **Focus on relationships, not marketing hype.**

☐ **Keep meaningful traditions and let troublesome ones go.**

☐ **Share the load. Invite friends to join your family to decorate the tree, do some group baking, and wrap gifts.**

☐ **Avoid contributing to others' clutter by giving consumables such as concert tickets, specialty items to eat and drink, bath treats, and coupons for services.**

☐ **Avoid busting your budget. Meaningful gifts are thoughtful and priceless.**

☐ **Instead of expensive and time-consuming decoration schemes, spruce up the house with live poinsettias, crafts the kids make, and candles.**

☐ **Delegate. Kids can wrap presents and your partner can set the table.**

☐ **Consider an informal, potluck dinner or opt for dinner reservations instead of cooking.**

☐ **Have realistic expectations regarding others. Personalities don't change just because it is Christmas.**

☐ **Don't throw out your schedule because of the holidays. If you usually take a daily walk, take it.**

☐ **Plan ahead.**

☐ **Listen to the music of the season. It feeds the soul.**

☐ **There is no perfect holiday. Relax and make it yours.**

SECTION THREE
Emotional Clutter

*Unfulfilling activities and the self-defeating thoughts
and feelings that keep us from our highest potential.*

Friends: Soul Mates or Spirit-vampires?

"The best thing to do behind someone's back is to pat it."
—WordsCanHeal.org newsletter

Anna is fun. She throws great parties and has an infectious "give 'em hell" attitude. But this gal has no sense of time. More than once, we'd make plans to meet for lunch or a movie and she'd leave me waiting, wondering if she'd fallen in front of a bus. Her tardiness made me mad. Damn mad. Even her bubbly personality and dazzling conversation couldn't compensate for the on-edge feeling I got when Anna suggested we get together. I felt controlled, unappreciated, and taken for granted. Although our friendship had its sunny moments, it was often drenched with broken commitments and unreliability. As time went on, the relationship soured. It had become unhealthy and toxic.

My friend Moe told me that she gets tense a few days before her weekly bridge game. "I feel a knot in my stomach. It's awful.

One of the gals I play with puts me on edge. I tiptoe around her and watch every word I say. When I'm with her, I feel like something's wrong with me."

Jan, another friend, told me that her friend Leigh tells the best stories. "The trouble is, they're usually about other people. Just listening to her makes me feel like a part of her nasty gossip."

The test of a relationship is how it makes us feel. Whether they're recent or well-aged, healthy friendships hum. They buoy us up when the load gets heavy and keep us steady when the rough waves hit. They nurture and console, inspire and encourage. Some are intimate soul-bonding affairs. Others are casual and activity focused. They might begin in preschool and last a lifetime, or burst on the scene, infuse life with a special energy and then, like a comet, fade and disappear. All have value and add texture to our lives.

But when relationships lack harmony, trust, or respect, when we feel anxious, belittled, or betrayed, when we can't relax, be ourselves, and act spontaneously, someone or something is out of tune.

"While toxic people account for 10 percent of the population, they're behind nearly 50 percent of damaged relationships," wrote author and human potential speaker Mike Moore. In "Coping with Difficult People," his special report on assertiveness, Mr. Moore warned that toxic people rob us of our dignity, destroy our confidence, and increase our stress levels. "They can make our lives hellish. We become less productive as our morale decreases. These people get away with it, because we let them."

Even if we realize that a relationship with a friend or family member is less than ideal, we may still remain involved, either by accepting what it is or hoping for a change. I asked human relations expert Harinder Dhillon about this. "There are so many reasons people stay in unhealthy relationships," she said. "They may retain a strong sense of loyalty even if they are betrayed. Or they may fear being abandoned and ending up alone. Others may even believe that they deserve harsh treatment. For some, it's a fear of how their community or social circle will react if they leave."

We might also play the "supporting cast" for a person who thrives on attention or suffer the patronizing put-downs of an insecure intellectual. Ms. Dhillon said that we should dig inside ourselves to understand why we attract these people or why they are attracted to us. "Sometimes we fear change and stay with the people we know, or we may lack clarity about who we are, how we feel, or what we want from life. This opens the door for others to define and control us," she said. "Chances are, our identities are somehow mixed in with theirs. And," she added, "toxic relationships can be a familiar family legacy."

Clinical social worker Mark Sichel maintains that toxic families often view those family members who develop their uniqueness and own interests as traitors to the family. "I have seen shocking rejection and abandoning of people [by their families of origin] if they become successful, psychologically evolved, healthy, and sober," Sichel wrote in "The Ties that Bind, The Ties that Strangle," an article for *Selfhelp* magazine.

We don't have to clutter our lives with relationships that threaten our happiness and sense of self-worth. We do have choices. "Set firm boundaries on what you will accept and be firm with others on where those boundaries are," Ms. Dhillon said. "This means standing up to those who push against them."

Confrontation is a good thing and is essential in healthy relationships. But it's not always easy. When facing up to a person with whom we have an unsatisfying relationship, Mr. Moore emphasizes that it is essential to show respect and "expect nothing less in return." He stresses to "make eye contact, stay calm, and don't argue. Just listen. Don't accuse. Just state how you feel and why. If things get out of hand, turn and walk away. You never have to take abuse. Clear, respectful, two-way communication keeps a relationship strong. It gives everyone a chance to focus on what's important."

Sometimes a situation can be so destructive that we may need to limit contact or even drop a relationship. This can be tough, especially if it involves someone with whom we share a long history. But it's quality and not the length of the relationship that matters. When things cease to be healthy, we have to preserve our mental and spiritual well-being. Toxic relationships and the harm that they bring can affect our lives so strongly that they make us sick.

Trent and Stella had such a relationship. Trent, a highly respected professional, struggled for twenty years to be the husband Stella wanted. Although this easygoing man was plagued by painful bouts of arthritis, he met the demands of work, rarely missed the kids' games, and encouraged his wife's outside interests. But it never seemed enough. "Stella wanted someone I wasn't, even though I turned myself inside out for her," he said. Eventually they separated.

Just four months after the couple parted, I saw someone who resembled Trent. I would have walked on by, but the man waved me over. It *was* Trent. I was stunned. Once overweight and rapidly aging, he had slimmed down and was decidedly sexy, a single girl's dream. His ever-present cane was gone and a wide, easy smile replaced the painful grimace that had haunted his face. "No drugs and no diet," he explained when I asked about his transformation. "I'm happy, plain and simple. Physically and spiritually, that marriage was killing me. We just weren't right for each other." Today he has a host of new friends and delights in interests that he had neglected for two decades. "It was hard adjusting, but now I've got me back. It feels good. Life is great. And Stella is happier, too."

Joan, sensing that a new acquaintance's needs would conflict with her own well-being, backed away from a potentially toxic relationship. "It was one of the most difficult things I ever did," she said. "This woman was in an abusive marriage with an alcoholic husband and needed someone to talk to. But her problems triggered unhappy memories I had of my first marriage. I told her I couldn't be her sounding board so I suggested she try a few sessions of Al-Anon [a program to support families of substance abusers]. I offered to pick her up and sit with her through the first few meetings. But she wouldn't go; she just wanted to unload. Although her situation was heartbreaking, I couldn't be her dumping ground. Suggesting Al-Anon was the best I could do for her and still take care of myself."

A life uncluttered with toxic relationships is a tall order. Providence seems to toss all sorts of challenges our way. But a walk on a sunny day, the unblemished innocence of a newborn, or the smell of spring blossoms affirms that life is a precious gift—too precious to squander even a minute of it in the mire of negative interactions and the company of spirit-vampires.

Healthy relationships resonate with harmony. They're dynamic, fun, and unwavering. They are loyal, gentle, and balanced. They're full of hearty hugs, surprise celebrations, and unconditional support. They're layered with love and laughter and they give and they take. And while they aren't all things at all times, they sweeten life like nothing else can. Caring friends are "earthly angels."

The rest—the folks who taint our souls and steal our joy—are simply clutter.

CLUTTER BUSTERS

☐ **Know yourself.** Define what qualities matter in your life and in your friends.

☐ **Do your homework.** Understand what makes a healthy relationship and why you might attract or be attracted to people who do not honor you.

☐ **Choose consciously.** Select friends with whom you can feel relaxed and natural.

☐ **Nurture relationships through open, assertive, honest communication.**

☐ **Dismiss difficult people who suck up time and energy.** Let go of people and activities that clutter life with negativity, stress, and feelings of obligations. Choose friends who inspire, nurture, or support your life's view.

☐ **Stand up for yourself.** Use direct, nonconfrontational language if someone is unkind, disrespectful, or abusive.

☐ **Bolster your self-esteem by taking an assertiveness course.**

☐ **Demand respect.** Dump the downers and pick positive, affirming relationships.

☐ **Avoid gossip.** If a tattler corrals you, let him or her know clearly and directly that you won't participate. Something as simple as "I don't want to talk about John" is often enough to thwart a gossiper.

☐ If you cannot improve an unhealthy relationship, you may need to limit contact. Get tough and vote with your feet if a situation remains toxic.

☐ Expect to go through withdrawal if you end a relationship. You have an empty place to fill. Look for someone who makes your day shine.

☐ While we don't have to embrace those who do us harm, we can understand that they might be acting out their own issues. We can forgive, but we don't have to forget. (See chapter 20 for more on forgiveness.)

☐ A positive attitude is contagious and a great negative-person deflector.

☐ Consider the support and assistance of a trained counselor.

CHAPTER **16**

Guilt: Unloading Our Burden Basket

"God will get you for that."
—Bea Arthur in the 1970s sitcom, *Maude.*

Guilt is one nasty creature. Nurtured by self-induced demands and self-blame, it clutters our lives with shoulds, shouldn't haves, and must nots. If we let it, guilt will bind us to a spit of unworthiness to roast over the coals of self-flagellation. This clever trickster puts us in conflict with ourselves as we play judge, jury, and transgressor.

Life seems so filled with shoulds. Family conventions might dictate that we send birthday and Christmas gifts to all of our relatives, even as the family expands faster than our budget. Our church might expect regular Sunday attendance, while we'd rather keep some of those days unplanned and for ourselves. Our inner critics might demand that our homes sparkle and our meals express artistic as well as culinary acumen, even though we hold nine-to-five jobs and have children to raise. While we're at it, incessantly nagging voices say we should care for aging parents, do our bit for the community, and, what the heck, save the planet, too.

While the shoulds needle us with expectations, the shouldn't haves clutter us with guilt about things we've already done. Sure, it might have been insensitive to forget a pal's birthday, irresponsible to send that payment late, and just plain dumb to overdo the tequila at the company party. Perhaps we shouldn't have lost our cool when our kid showed up wearing a spiked dog collar and multicolored hair. Unless we're born under a halo, chances are these and future bloopers will punctuate our lives.

Why is it that so many of life's harmless pleasures—wolfing down a second slice of cheesecake or doing absolutely nothing for an entire weekend—leave us with a naughty residue of guilt? Why do we feel guilty over things we did or didn't do? And how does guilt clutter our lives?

I decided to ask my 94-year-old neighbor, Alice. But this whirling dervish, with a packed-to-the-minute schedule, couldn't see me until four days later. While we sat in her living room nibbling salmon sandwiches and homemade fruitcake washed down with good, strong tea, she told me of tough times on the Saskatchewan prairies during the 1920s. She spoke of her husband, Art, and how he had courted her during the lean years of the Depression. We talked of family, friends, and the neighborhood they have lived in since moving to the West Coast in 1947. Through it all, I searched to understand how Alice dealt with life's challenges. In nearly a century of living, she must have shoveled her share of miseries.

We talked about the internal clutter that hounds so many of us—worry, envy, grudge holding, and, of course, guilt. Alice thoughtfully considered my questions. When she spoke, she offered no-nonsense, prairie wisdom. "I can't really say I've been bothered too much by those things. I'm thankful for what life gives me and I do my best to forgive and forget. If I have things to do, I get them done. As best I can, I mind my own business. As for guilt, I feel it's best to be honest and frank with others. If we do our best and mean well, we can't feel guilty, now can we?"

Alice's philosophy, as straightforward as the rows of peas and beans she and Art once grew in the vegetable garden, reflects an enviable peace of mind. As I studied Alice's lively and still lovely face, I felt that life's mental and spiritual burdens had somehow passed her by. Or, I wondered, had she bypassed them? Perhaps that is why Alice is still buzzing around like a woman of half her age.

For many of us, life is not so straightforward. Messages of right and wrong, planted by the media, religious dogma, and well-intentioned parents and teachers, seem to burrow right into our center, becoming an unrelenting, life-long jury of inner critics. Guilt clutters our hearts and souls with feelings of unworthiness and disappointment. We might ache over letting others down, wishing we had done more. We might fear punishment for the mistakes we've made and arm ourselves against real or imagined revenge. Or, thinking that others must see us as unworthy of friendship, we withdraw from life and lead lonely lives, where depression, drugs, and drink lie in wait.

Self-blame, an insidious source of internal clutter, is guilt's unforgiving accomplice. How often do we overlook or downplay the transgressions of others, while thrashing ourselves when we fall off the rails?

We may even feel guilty without actually being guilty. I felt chewed up inside when I missed a good friend's wedding. We've been pals since our diaper days, saw bell-bottoms and miniskirts come and go, and bucked up each other when our first marriages bit the dust. Now, after many years on her own, my buddy was taking a second plunge, and it was going to be some party. Just two days before her big day, the airline I was booked on fell into receivership. Along with hundreds of others, I wasn't going anywhere. Although the situation was beyond me, I blamed myself anyway.

Divorced parents know the guilt that comes from hurting others, especially their children. It can insidiously pressure us to bend when we should stand firm. I think of Emil, who, even though divorced twenty years ago, cannot refuse his grown daughter's requests. She asks, he gives. "I can't shake the feeling that I robbed her of the family she deserves. I let her down. Even though I know she takes advantage of me, I can't say no."

Sometimes, feelings of guilt have nothing at all to do with us. During a weekend retreat I attended many years ago, I met a truly brave soul whose son was serving a life sentence for murder. I did my best to understand how she felt—that she had failed as a mother. Throughout the few days we spent together, I watched her struggle to understand that her son, not her, was responsible for what had happened.

Guilt can also flower when the expectations of others are out of step with our personal values or needs. Is it truly a sin to forgo a family funeral or memorial service in favor of a personal, solitary remembrance, or to choose a common-law marriage over one that is legally sanctioned? Should we stay in a loveless or abusive relationship because our religious tradition or family expectations put thumbs down on divorce? While the answers to these questions require probing deeply within ourselves, we must seek to resolve our conflicts and affirm our duty to live life with inner integrity.

Guilt flourishes when we think that we've acted selfishly. The truly *selfish*, like the guy who hogs the bathroom or those who party through the night without considering their neighbors, are self-absorbed and dismiss the needs of others. It's all about them. The *selfless* put themselves at the end of the line. Even if they have an early morning appointment, they wouldn't dream of asking the partygoers next-door to turn down the music. Those who occupy the middle ground of healthy *self-interest* bypass guilt for personal integrity, which honors others and ourselves. It recognizes that we count. It lets us train for that marathon or devote a weekend entirely to ourselves while being mindful of—but not acquiescing to—the expectations of others. Healthy self-interest is the act of establishing boundaries that let our spirit shine. It is about nurturing our unique potential so we can offer others our greatest gifts, and, in doing so, create balanced, dynamic relationships.

By acknowledging that it is so very human to make faulty judgments, hurt others unintentionally, or fail to be everything to everyone, we can lighten up and exchange a verdict of guilt for what British psychotherapist Windy Dryden calls "constructive remorse." Guilt, he purports, is a rigid attitude that brands us as just plain bad instead of wonderfully and humanly imperfect. Constructive remorse challenges us to understand why we feel guilty, learn from our wrongdoings, and make amends to those we may have hurt. It says we are fallible and lets us accept our actions and improve on them. It does not punish, hold grudges, or brand us forever defective, and it lets us get on with life.

Beth Skala talks of the Native American's burden basket. "It's the mental and spiritual clutter we carry. Our burden basket contains regrets, unfilled wishes, addictions, failures, memories of abuse, unresolved issues, and guilt. We can bend under its weight as life tosses more in, or we can set it down and examine what's in it and choose to unload some of the weight."

The choice is ours.

CLUTTER BUSTERS

☐ See guilt as a wake-up call that something in your life needs attention. Take time to examine why you feel guilty. Practicing yoga or meditation opens us to what is happening inside ourselves. Answers emerge in stillness and silence.

☐ Accept that we make mistakes and see them as opportunities to learn and grow.

☐ Take responsibility for your mistakes. Make amends whenever possible.

☐ Replace self-blame with forgiveness.

☐ What may be true for others may not fit your value system. Express your integrity by living your own truth.

☐ We are not responsible for the lives of others. Offer help when it is requested but resist interfering with the life choice of others.

☐ Recognize when others are using guilt to manipulate and control us.

☐ Life is a gift. Live it joyfully by developing your talents and asserting your right to be happy.

17

No Doubt about Self-doubt

"Beautiful young people are an accident of nature.
Beautiful old people are works of art."
—Eleanor Roosevelt

A svelte model, radiant in a single digit-size dress, smiled seductively from a page of a glossy women's magazine. I scrutinized her computer-enhanced complexion, jet-set tresses, and—I couldn't help but notice—a butt the size of a walnut. I admitted that she looked great. Bold type swirled about her, taunting me.

"Win the Makeover of Your Life!"

"Swing into Style with an Exciting New Wardrobe!"

"Shape up with Personalized Fitness Training!"

"Be the Woman You Always Wanted to Be!"

Gosh, I am the woman I want to be; at least I thought I was until I contemplated that perfectly coiffed, smugly confident image. Perhaps I could use a bit of pruning and shaping. Rock-hard abs and a set of Britney's showstoppers would top up the old bod just fine. Maybe I should "push 'em up and stick 'em out," get a nip and tuck, and strut, strut, strut my stuff? And that contest? Hmmm, I just might give it some thought.

With dimpling thighs and the beginning of a second chin, it's no surprise that my confidence quotient is a bit shaky. It takes tough self-talk and far too many sweaty hours at the gym to silence the inner critics and keep the spirit (and a whole lot more) from sagging. But hey, people at any age and size are keeping it together. For every 5'10", 110-pound mutant, there are legions of others slurping lattes (with extra cream, thank you very much). They're meeting life head-on. Right?

Well, sort of.

While we might convince ourselves that we wouldn't change places with Britney, whispers of self-doubt wiggle into our souls, murmuring subtle messages that we're about as sexy as a hive of hostile bees. And self-doubt attacks more than the image we see in the mirror; it can sabotage our willingness to step out from the shadows and take on life. When our confidence is rattled we might resist moving to a new town, upgrading our education, or standing up to a bullying boss. While others may influence how we view ourselves, we're the ones who thrust our doubts deep into our souls.

Self-doubters tend to dismiss compliments and embrace criticisms. They focus—even highlight—their weaknesses, ensuring that others see their shortcomings as clearly as they do. Eleanor Roosevelt's clever one-liner "No one can make you feel inadequate without your permission" says it all.

Like dust bunnies on cleaning day, self-doubt can creep from out of nowhere to destroy our potential for rich and meaningful lives. Self-doubt creates life-limiting feelings of envy of those who succeed, sadness over our loss of fulfillment, and anxiety about tomorrow. It can cause us to retreat from life and replace its mystery and excitement with regrets and bitterness. We might hesitate to speak up if we are unfairly attacked, shy away from social occasions that could stimulate new friendships, or pass over promotion opportunities.

Feelings of self-doubt are epidemic. It's a top-to-bottom, classless affliction. "Self-doubt is rampant in our culture, even among those who appear most successful," said psychologist Dr. Mary Louise Reilly. "I work with some top-notch professionals who appear to have it all together, yet don't see themselves as successful. They often feel like frauds, not worthy of what they've accomplished." She explains that we can't see our successes or even hear the accolades we justly deserve when disapproving internal voices shout them down.

Dr. Reilly spoke of a consultant who is a wizard at conjuring brilliant proposals yet quakes at presenting them and a silver-tongued salesperson who can sell bytes to Bill Gates yet shrinks at asking for a raise. "Their prospects are limited by inner voices that say, 'I can't do this,' instead of, 'This is a challenge I will conquer.'"

When our minds are a flurry of nay-saying, self-doubt clutters our spirit, making it easy to disconnect from others and miss the splendors around us. That magical pause just before the sun sets and the welcoming promise of new opportunities can be lost under negative rumblings. Dr. Reilly said that we're often the architects of our own misery. "We have to stop heaping abuse on ourselves. We get up in the morning, look in the mirror, and start in. And this can go on all day."

■ ■ ■

Instead of focusing on our real or imagined defects, we need to appreciate ourselves, double chins and all. That might mean taking baby steps by paying attention to the verbal and non-verbal messages others give us. Highlight the positive. A smile, an invitation for coffee, a request for a recipe, or a call just to say hello confirm that we are valued.

While self-doubt is a tenacious monster, it withers in the presence of success. Janet is a paragon of confidence, but it didn't come easy. "Ten years ago I started life over from scratch in a new city with two kids I was raising by myself," she said. "The job market was tight, so I decided to go back to university and upgrade. I was scared to death. It had been ages since I had been a student. My mind reeled with reasons why I'd fail. I was terrified of falling flat on my face."

Although Janet had dabbled in community center courses while raising her children, this was a dive into the deep end. Research papers required pesky footnotes. There were presentations to make in front of students half her age, and the battle for marks with those agile, young minds was keen. She also had to juggle part-time jobs and the children's needs with class schedules and study time. But she hung on—and finished. "I often felt defeated, like I'd never make it. But getting that degree was like doing the Boston Marathon. I was exhausted, but boy, did it feel good, not just because I had done it but because I had overcome an enormous inner hurdle. I can do anything now." Instead of letting self-doubt clutter her life, Janet has become one empowered, go-get-'em gal.

Jim, a whiz-bang political advisor, was born with the confidence Janet had earned, or so it seemed. Nothing could shake this young man. At just twenty-five years of age, he could saunter into a boardroom of strangers like it was a backyard barbeque. Yet when an offer to work for a high-profile government official landed in his lap, he hesitated. "I was truly flattered, but I had waves of uncertainty—huge ones. The man I was to work for was extremely bright, extremely capable, and unbelievably demanding. I was young for this sort of job and knew I could be setting myself up to bomb out."

Jim marched into the arena anyway. "After some hesitation I decided not to awfulize the situation. I wasn't going to let my insecurities control me. After all, I figured that life is about taking chances, so I convinced myself that this was an opportunity to transcend my limits." And he did. Today Jim advises top-level politicians.

Jim's gutsy attitude inspired me. I vowed to silence the interior voices that nattered on about aging faces and sagging body parts, and I decided to have it out with the woman in the mirror.

I looked closely at my reflection. The face I saw reminded me of an ancient Chinese vase I had examined in a course I had taken. The vase's surface was cobwebbed with delicate, fine lines. A small chip marred the rim. "The chip says it has a history—it knows life," said our instructor, Patricia Kidd. "The tiny lines on the surface are known as crackle. These 'caresses of time' add to its beauty and," said Ms. Kidd, turning the vase lovingly, "they increase its value."

Oh, I liked that.

I peered deeper into the mirror, scrutinizing the crackle creeping across my face—my very own "caress of time." Beautiful? Well, I'm not sure about that. But Ms. Kidd's words made me realize how vital it is to reframe how we see our imperfections—inner ones as well as those in the mirror—and question the standards that measure personal worth, success, and yes, even beauty. Like that little vase, perhaps we need to shift from judgment to acceptance—of others and ourselves—and let go of the mental and soul-shattering clutter that self-doubt breeds.

CLUTTER BUSTERS

- ☐ Resist heaping negative thoughts on yourself. Boost your self-esteem by making a Brag Sheet that lists all of your wonderful qualities.

- ☐ Have realistic goals. You may bomb as the leader of the country but make one heck of a community organizer.

- ☐ Live your own life and tune out the expectations of others. Be a dog-walker, bus driver, or opera diva if that's your dream.

- ☐ Praise yourself when you make the grade. Let your buddies in on the good news.

- ☐ Resist self-deprecating language. Putting yourself or your abilities down colors how others see you.

- ☐ Keep a journal or write a letter to yourself expressing your fears. Give yourself advice on how to overcome them.

- ☐ Prove you are loveable by acting loving. Cross the street to greet a new neighbor. Be the first to say hello when you meet someone. Asking a newcomer to coffee could seed a new friendship.

- ☐ Whether or not you plan to speak in public, consider participating in a Toastmasters' course. It is an excellent way to meet people and build confidence.

☐ Take positive steps. Replacing dessert with an after-dinner walk will clear your head and trim the waistline, creating a feel-good attitude.

☐ Persevere. As Thomas Edison once said, "I haven't failed. I've just found ten thousand ways that won't work."

☐ If feelings of self-doubt severely limit your life, consider speaking with a trained professional.

18

Don't Worry. Be Happy

*"What lies behind us and what lies before us are
tiny matters compared to what lies within us."*

As I stroll through my garden contemplating the apple trees in
blossom, I think of the juicy orbs that will soon bend their
branches. Under them summer flowers will stretch their way
toward the sun. When the season fades, their seeds will spill into
the soil and rest, waiting to repeat nature's predictable cycle.
These plants—the apple trees and the flowers that grow under
them—flourish in a state of trusting acceptance.

But life is not so effortless with us. When we don't know what
to expect or can't understand or control a situation, worry rattles
our innards. It makes us prisoners of phantom suspicions that
can infiltrate the broader landscape of life. Like the steady drone
of traffic in rush hour, worry hums away in the mind, drowning out

the music of today and cluttering our life with uncertainty and stress. Yet worrying seems to be a universal pastime. In some cultures, it's expected. A friend's Jewish mother considers it her duty to brood over her family. How better to show she cares? It's a way of life for Greek elders to click and clack their worry beads as they wait in airport lounges or linger over afternoon coffee. And worry is in every parent's job description.

As my children morphed from turbulent teenagers to young adults studying away from home, I held my breath, praying that the choices they made would further their dreams and not send them tumbling back with broken lives and empty pockets. Even though there were no causes for concern, I still caught myself wondering how Carley would handle her next biology exam, and I envisioned all sorts of calamities if David, an aspiring chef, decided to party hearty instead of perfecting his hollandaise sauce. Couldn't they just keep their heads in the books, eat something green occasionally, floss, and call home on Sundays?

"At its worst, worry can be a relentless scavenger, roaming the corners of your mind, feeding on anything, never leaving you alone," Edward Hallowell wrote in his book *Worry: Hope and Help for a Common Condition*. Hallowell suggested that continual worry is a "disease of the imagination" that overshadows life and sabotages our capacity to work, love, and play.

If we let it, our minds can become so saturated with what-ifs that we retreat from life. I think of two friends, Mark and Sonja, who, betrayed by their former spouses, are fearful of loving again. Each worries about repeating the pain in their past relationships. "I'd like to meet someone nice, someone good," said Sonja, yet she keeps her life closed to all but a few married female friends.

Mark worries that he'll let a new partner down and that he can't succeed in a relationship and, like Sonja, avoids intimacy.

But worry is not all bad. It's the body's way to alert us to potential problems and signal when a situation demands attention or action. Worry can prompt us to get safety information before we hike the backcountry, call the doctor if we notice sudden changes in our health, make preparations if we live in an area prone to natural disasters, and take a closer look at potential lovers.

While the scope for worry is wide and deep, we usually feel most troubled by situations we can't influence. Like sunshine on sunflowers, knowledge illuminates the shadows where worry skulks. In my husband's business as a financial planner, he sees clients overcome with worry, often over financial insecurity when they retire. He tells me that it's common for clients with healthy resources to feel as troubled as those with lighter pockets. One well-heeled client, he said, was convinced that he'd spend his old age sleeping over hot-air vents in public parks. "We looked over his situation and found that not only could he retire in style but he could do it years sooner. When he understood this and could see past his imagined fears, his relief was instantaneous."

While understanding that our fears help combat worry, taking action finishes the job. Instead of being obsessed about cancer, we can get regular checkups and kick-start our days with brisk walks instead of tanking up on caffeine and nicotine. If our job is at risk, we can learn new skills. Instead of losing sleep fretting about whether the car will get us to work tomorrow, we can make an appointment with a mechanic. Seeking financial advice, picking up a phrase book before setting off to Italy, or talking with a professional about why love went bad gives us the power to attack the roots of worry and clear the mental clutter it breeds.

But we often procrastinate or avoid issues, so our problems hang around, spawning more worry—and more inner clutter. A friend of mine beats these beasts by making worry appointments. "If something's on my mind, I book a time to deal with it. Doing this stops the problem from dominating the day. And if I can't solve it then, I book another appointment."

Getting off of our butts also helps. Nothing clears internal clutter like the rush of feel-good endorphins ignited by exercise. Many find that the gentle movements of yoga and tai chi focus the mind in the present moment. Walking works wonders, whatever the weather. Our troubles seem less threatening when we trip through leaf-laced streets in October, tramp through December's snowflakes, or amble through the neighborhood on a summer evening.

Laughter also puts things in perspective. "I'm Xena the Worrier Princess," said May Brown, a humor writer and stand-up comic. "To combat my worries, I take a situation to the ridiculous." As an example, she said that if she were writing a book and lost confidence in it, she'd tell herself, "When it's published, Oprah will start a Worst Book of the Month Club and I'll be her first guest. Then everyone will know I'm a fraud and I'll lose my house, the car, and the cat, and be left to eke out a living as a bag lady. Then I'll starve and die alone with just the memory of my cat for company. Before long, I realize how silly my worries are and start chuckling. It's pretty hard to feel down when we're laughing."

It also helps to let go of things and people we can't control. Worrying about a friend who smokes a pack a day, guzzles too many martinis, or lives on corner-store take-out clutters our lives, not theirs. Yes, it hurts to see those we care about make poor or harmful choices, but the consequences belong to them. And that goes for our kids, too. I can't write Carley's exams or control my son's yen for adventure, but I can offer guidance and share the lessons I've learned. If they choose to stumble into the potholes that once tripped me up, I must remember that it's their stumble and their opportunity to learn and maybe even build a little character. Of course, it's legitimate to support those whose lives are disrupted by disabilities or life traumas, but even then, we must let ourselves off the worry hook once we've done what we can.

For many of us, faith helps. Whether it is Buddhist meditation, a Gregorian chant, or a heartfelt reading of a Biblical psalm, prayer rests the mind. The Serenity Prayer, which directs us to ask God to "grant me the Serenity to accept the things I cannot change, courage to change the things I can, and wisdom to know the difference," has helped millions. Some join prayer groups that provide a feeling of connectedness as they support each other over life's bumps.

We'll have clear, uncluttered space in our minds and hearts if we yank out the stubborn roots of worry. We need to hoe our own row and not that of others, separate the facts from fantasies, and take constructive action. Uncluttering the mind of the what-ifs of worry is ultimately about perspective—knowing what's within our control and letting go of what isn't. As a 112-year-old man said in explaining the secret to his long life, "When it rains, I just let it."

CLUTTER BUSTERS

☐ Define the problem. If this is difficult, talk it out with a friend or counselor or consult the list of books in Resources.

☐ Accept that some troublesome problems and situations cannot be changed, but we can change our attitudes about them.

☐ If the situation is not your responsibility, offer help and then let it go.

☐ Get the facts. Assumptions and what-ifs create needless worry.

☐ Worry is a state of indecision. Seek solutions.

☐ Don't procrastinate. Take constructive action as soon as possible.

☐ Work out your worry. Exercise feeds mental and physical health.

☐ Laugh every day. Worry festers in a serious soul. Read *Lighten Up: Survival Skills for People under Pressure* (listed in Resources) for ways to use humor to eject worry.

☐ Recognize daily blessings. Worry abhors optimism and gratitude.

☐ Get sufficient rest. Sleep deprivation affects all aspects of health, especially your mental outlook.

■ ■ ■

☐ **Seek reassurance from friends and professionals.**

☐ **Try meditation or meditative exercise such as yoga or tai chi.**

☐ **You've gotta have faith. Look to your God for guidance.**

CHAPTER 19

Money Matters:
For What It's Worth

"The more you know, the less you need."
—Australian Aboriginal saying

We love it and we despise it. We treat it with polite disdain, yet dream of winning the Big One. Whatever the circumstances, our relationship with money is a convoluted, lifelong affair. Whether we slurped our pabulum from a silver spoon or we leave this life in a plain, pine box, while we live, money can tease and tantalize and seduce and nurture.

What fun and what fear—and what internal clutter—it can generate. By nurturing greed and envy, it can destroy contentment with what we already have. Even while we may feel satisfied with our lot in life, who has not drooled over a friend's nifty new outfit or a neighbor's plans for an extended winter holiday?

We also experience the dark side of the coin when money is used to control others, such as a working spouse depriving his or her stay-at-home partner of personal funds or a parent taunting an adult child with an inheritance. And when it comes to divorce, money is often a foil for a power struggle: the partner who gets the most, wins, whatever the residue effects on each other or the children.

Money can also generate worry, anxiety, and fear. With consumer debt at record levels in North America, many are vulnerable to potential instability through job loss or illness. And as for the future? Will we become a lost soul living with our worldly goods stuffed into bags as we toddle from park bench to park bench?

George Garner, a middle-aged, senior executive with a Canadian financial institution, knows about concern for the future. Although he earns a six-figure income, owns a holiday cottage, and takes regular vacations, he told me that one of his biggest fears is not having enough when he retires. He is not alone. Security in our old age is a prime concern for most of us, whatever our income. Statistics say that most of us will find retirement a struggle. While Mr. Garner acknowledged this fear in his own life, he said that the best way to avoid anxiety is to start saving early, in whatever meager fashion. "Most of us don't think about retirement until we are in our forties and fifties, and that's getting a bit late. Achieving peace of mind might mean putting yourself in a fairly uncomfortable position while someone shows you your true financial picture. Then you can see what you need to do to achieve a comfortable level."

He said that if he were really struggling financially he would consider moving from Toronto to a less expensive community.

"Life is a series of choices. We choose to live where we live and spend what we spend. It's a matter of taking responsibility. But in the end, financial comfort is largely a state of mind," he concurred, "whatever the size of the pile."

Nancy McKinstry, a financial advisor for more than twenty years, had a pragmatic message when it comes to uncluttering the money issues in our lives. "I see the same concerns with clients who have $2 million as with those with $2,000. We need to take a realistic assessment of our needs and understand what resources we have." She offered two ways to resolve our financial affairs: make more or spend less. "Consider all your expenses," she said. "How many are discretionary? Can you give less expensive presents, reduce entertainment costs, eat at home more often? Do you need to fund your adult children? What about the gas-guzzling SUV and the club memberships? Can you curb impulsive spending?"

If our spending is under control and we are still scrounging to pay the rent, Ms. McKinstry provided this advice: "Learn how to make more. You can improve your employment skills or look for a job that offers better compensation. Regular, disciplined investing helps, too. Of course, you can always marry well . . . whatever it takes," she added with a chuckle.

While concerns about money can clutter our internal world, it can also create chaos in our back pockets. A wallet filled with credit cards means a stack of bills to manage each month. Peace of mind can whirl out of control as we become entangled in a maze of decisions, that, if made poorly, can result in late payments, interest charges, bad credit, and fear that the next knock on the door heralds a collection agent.

Psychologist David Benner had another point of view on financial freedom. In his book *Money Madness and Financial Freedom*, Dr. Benner wrote that "financial freedom is often confused with occupational freedom. . . . We can retire on a healthy pension and still obsess about money issues." He noted that "financial freedom is freedom to see money for what it is, to use it in ways that constructively enhance life for yourself and others. . . . True financial freedom is independent of wealth." Like George Garner, Dr. Benner supported the notion that financial freedom is a matter of attitude, not a bank balance.

Patti and David, middle-income earners who live on the Canadian West Coast, put aside savings each month for retirement but invest just as earnestly in life experiences. Patti takes regular trips to visit family and friends, and each autumn they both scoot off to France or Italy for the better part of a month.

"Our friends ask how we can afford to travel so often. It's not like we have big incomes or a magic formula," said Patti. "We focus on what matters to us. We don't eat out much and we don't smoke. Dave makes our wine, and the car I drive is still dependable after thirteen years. We usually entertain at home. Cultural traveling is our thing—that's where our money goes. When we're away, we shop at the markets and get right into the regional cuisine. And we take all the time we want in cafés and art museums. During the rest of year, we prepare for the next trip. This winter I'll be practicing my French while Dave cooks up some of regional recipes we've discovered. Financial freedom is all about priorities, I guess."

And choices.

"I work three days a week," said a caller to a radio show I tuned in to one afternoon. The speaker, a middle-aged man, talked about how practicing his profession as a dentist part-time allowed time for a hobby: making stained-glass art.

"It's become a second job. I have pieces in churches and buildings downtown. It feels great." He went on to say that soldering and grinding glass were just as fulfilling as drilling his patients' teeth. "For me, life is an ideal combination of art and science, but to have this, I live simply. You wouldn't believe how little I live on."

Later that day I thought about what this dentist/craftsman had said. He had consciously chosen his lifestyle. He talked of driving a car "that doesn't turn any heads" and living far below the economic standard of his colleagues. But the calmness in his voice and the quiet satisfaction in how he described his life made me pause as I realized that his life focus was not about making money but making life *his*.

However large or small our financial portfolios are, it is how we define the *enough* quotient that determines our level of happiness. To the distressed it might be enough to have a sympathetic friend; to the hungry, a hot meal. Author and adventurer Colin Angus and his two friends found that "enough" was a shoestring budget scraped together to finance a rafting trip down the length of the Amazon River. The team became the first to complete the excursion without loss of life. The men then tackled Mongolia's Yenisey, the world's last unchallenged river. Their next trip will take them from Vancouver to Moscow, a five-month ordeal to be done solely by human power. While Mr. Angus publishes his adventures and documents them on film for presentations, it is not fame or fortune that motivates him but the gripping thrill of challenging nature. For Colin, "enough" is what it takes to facilitate his next adventure.

For Chuck, a Wisconsin college professor and food bank volunteer, the answer is not so clear. "It is easy to philosophize about how much is enough, but living that philosophy is another story," he said. We talked about his wife, Deanna, who devotes six weeks each year to teaching in Cambodia, a country rife with poverty and political uncertainty. For most Cambodians, as with many who live in dire circumstances, having enough is measured against what is possible.

"If a person is poor, as many of my wife's students and my food bank clients are, they hope for a life with more than just the basic needs. But I don't think that will ultimately make them happy, for there is the natural tendency to want more, and then more again." He told me about how he spends several weeks each year in an Indian ashram. "I live without electricity, TV, radio, and newspapers. A room to sleep in, food to eat, and activities keep me satisfied. But to work and earn a decent wage is satisfying, too. I believe contentment is found in being mindful of what we have—all the time—for the material things we desire may never come our way." Reflecting on Chuck's words, I realized that money cannot buy yesterday. Money-making demands that we surrender time, that finite resource we cannot replace. If we consciously choose how we spend our life's time, we are on the track of a tailor-made life—one that nurtures our deepest joys. When we leave this life, it won't matter if the bed we lie on is covered in silk or sackcloth if the life we led was rich in experiences and human connection.

Understanding that our net worth is *not* our personal worth removes us from the "get-more" treadmill and halts the clutter it breeds. Appreciating what we have, celebrating the good fortune of others, and embracing our rainbow of blessings illuminates life. As with Colin and Patti and David, when money is used to connect us to the rich potential of the human experience, we've got it all, whatever the number on the bottom line of our bank statement.

C L U T T E R   B U S T E R S

- [ ] Whether it's a trip to France, learning a language, or developing a new skill, do what makes your life hum.

- [ ] Media contrives to foster envy. Tune out the adman; he hawks discontent, not happiness.

- [ ] Give yourself the gift of a Blessings Book and update it daily with all that made your day special: a conversation with a friend, a parking spot close to your destination, a drawing done by your child just for you, an appointment that went well, a new client, a coworker who offered assistance, or a great cappuccino at the end of the day.

- [ ] Be generous and share what you have, be it a surplus of garden vegetables, time to serve in the community, a donation to a charity, or a smile to a stranger.

- [ ] Recognize that financial freedom is about attitude, not a number in a bank account.

- [ ] Limit paper clutter by streamlining your financial matters.

- [ ] Invest in your future by finding a trusted advisor to analyze your financial picture and help you establish realistic goals.

- [ ] Read. While research on the psychology of money is limited, the books mentioned in Resources have valuable, life-changing insights.

Nudge That Grudge

*"Every man should keep a fair-sized cemetery
in which to bury the faults of his friends."*
—Henry Ward Beecher, U.S. abolitionist and clergyman

A friend unintentionally breaks an heirloom vase, a good buddy forgets your birthday, and another cancels a date. Unless we talk it out, these folks may not know they've crossed our foul line, and the gripe remains ours, lodged in our hearts to fester and froth. Relationships can dissolve if we nurture real or imagined slights.

Hate poisons the soul, but love and forgiveness enrich it, Robert Lawrence Smith wrote in A *Quaker Book of Wisdom.* Just as material clutter can dominate our physical space, resentments and grudges can commandeer space in our hearts and spirits, forcing out loving thoughts and positive emotions.

If our internal world fills with the chatter that replays the hurts of yesterday, the sounds of harmony—"the voice of God"—

is muffled. We can eclipse our peace of mind with life-deadening thoughts. Over time, unresolved grudges can lead to spiritual suicide by destroying tomorrow's joys while feeding yesterday's hurts. They leave us mired in the past as today gallops by. Fearing future hurts, we might hole up in a guarded and closed existence, sacrificing the freedom to live spontaneously and truly be ourselves.

Families are a fertile soil for grudges. My friend Myrna harbored such intense resentment toward her sister (they both eyed the same guy, but Myrna scored the wedding ring) that it severed ties between them. As the years passed, they missed important milestones as nieces and nephews grew, graduated, and married. It took their father's death twenty-seven years later and a few rounds of bourbon after the funeral before Myrna dropped the past.

Another friend who lived several thousand miles from her family home chose not to harbor a grudge when her two sisters divided their mother's heirlooms between them on her death. "By the time I got home it was all over. Wonderful pieces of decorative china, the silver set, Mom's rings and jewelry—all gone," she said. "I was mighty upset for a time but eventually decided it wasn't worth heckling over."

Divorce is also a playground for grudges. "Claire talks as if Sam is still in the next room," reported a concerned friend after a visit with a divorced buddy of ours. "She hasn't heard from him in ten years but still goes on about how he fooled around on her." Claire's hurt and seething animosity toward Sam keeps her in the loop—his loop. Around and around she goes, inflicting the present with yesterday's pain.

And what about the kids? Too often grudges between spouses, especially ex-spouses, seem to ensnare the little ones. As Mom and Dad recant tomes of bitter history, the innocents feel their parents' confusion and anger. They want and need to love each parent. Their own mental well-being depends on it. Yet as the big folks attack each other, the little ones feel the pain.

What holds us back from confronting issues directly when they're fresh and unseasoned? Why do we turn today's issues into tomorrow's grudges? Perhaps we feel that our grudge is justified. It might feel good to serve up an order of blame, especially if we can season it with a little guilt. And who knows? A side order of revenge might be on the menu, too. But the payback for us is a dose of negative clutter that infiltrates our minds and hearts.

Science is fast acknowledging that our happiness and health could depend on letting go of our grudges and checklists of the wrongdoings of others. Cancer researchers Carl Simonton and James Creighton argue that changing our attitudes in a positive direction is one of the most powerful options we have in maintaining good health. Other research indicates that when we consciously shift from a negative to a positive emotion, our heart rhythms immediately change. This affects the brain, creating a cascade of internal events that can actually reverse the effects of stress, boost our ability to think clearly, and benefit the entire body by increasing overall health, vitality, and emotional stability.

Helen Kaplan Singer, M.D. agrees. She documented that negative thoughts penetrate our psyche and our bodies. Blame, anger, and hostility—all feelings associated with grudge holding—can wreak havoc on blood pressure, increase vulnerability to heart disease, reduce immune system efficiency, and—this deserves a headline—contribute to sexual dysfunction.

We need to dump grudges, ditch resentments, and get on with the good things in life. But how?

Sometimes the answer is just down the street. "We need to rant, get down, and really vent," my friend Jessica stressed during one of our weekly chats. "There's nothing like a darn-good bitch session. Then you gotta let go and move on."

Psychologist Dr. James Pennebaker concurs. In his book *Opening Up: The Healing Power of Expressing Emotions* Pennebaker stressed that talking out our grievances can "change the ways we think and feel about traumatic events and about ourselves." We should also pick up a pen and paper. Pennebaker's work in journal therapy examines how writing about emotional upheaval has improved the physical and mental health of children, nursing-home residents, arthritis sufferers, students, and even rape victims.

Others feel that forgiveness is the answer. Psychotherapist Frederic Luskin of Stanford University's Forgiveness Project likened grudges to airplanes forever circling on our radar screen. He used the metaphor of a plane to explain the energy it takes to keep them flying forever. "Those planes can circle for years, dominating our lives and affecting everyone in it. Forgiveness is letting the plane land," said Dr. Luskin, who has taught courses on forgiveness in troubled regions such as Northern Ireland.

Easy to say, yet forgiving someone who has deeply wounded us can be a near impossible task. "Forgiveness is a gift to someone who may not deserve it. It means understanding the other's perspective and trying to empathize with them," said Charlotte vanOyen Witvliet, who researches forgiveness at Hope College in Michigan.

"Forgiveness is a two-step process of first chipping away at that crusty layer of bitterness and then replacing it with compassion. It takes moral muscle and tremendous courage, but this difficult path ultimately leads to life," said Dr. Witvliet. "We all fall short in different ways and all are in need of grace. Of course, it helps if the offender shows a measure of contrition, a bit of remorse for the hurt they've caused."

But don't count on it. Not everyone is going to fess up. If we hold back our forgiveness until the offender shows sincere remorse, we risk becoming prisoners to our bitter, hurtful feelings. Then we empower those who wish to hurt us.

It's difficult to believe that the victims of Timothy McVeigh's bombing will ever forget the day in Oklahoma when they lost loved ones, nor will they forget McVeigh's lack of remorse. Nor should they. While forgiveness allows us to understand and put hurt in perspective, it does not mean condoning, excusing, or forgetting, nor does it require reconciliation, especially if the situation was abusive. It's an inside thing, a letting go of our bitterness, not for their sake but for ours. Otherwise these nasty blokes move in and, as Dr. Luskin put it, "rent space in our minds."

Anyone who angers you, conquers you, wrote Rabbi Charles Klein. In his wonderful book, *How to Forgive When You Can't Forget*, Rabbi Klein counseled us to put the hurt in perspective, resist judging others, and acknowledge human failings.

While the actions of another may be intended to hurt us, we may not understand that person's motivation. It might be a reaction to a situation that has nothing to do with us, or the person may suffer from depression, envy, or a personality dis-order such as narcissism. Understanding this allows us to view the situation with compassion, not anger. Sure, it can be tough to put hurt behind us, but our mental, spiritual and physical health depends on it.

And that is reason enough.

C L U T T E R   B U S T E R S

Dr. Frederic Luskin, author of *Forgive for Good*, offers nine steps to forgiveness. These are summarized from his Web site with permission.

1. **Know exactly how you feel about the troubling incident and discuss it with a trusted person.**

2. **Commit to taking action to feel better. Forgiveness is for you and not for anyone else.**

3. **Forgiveness does not mean reconciling or condoning the action.**

4. **Get the right perspective on what is happening. Recognize that your distress comes from hurt feelings and thoughts and the physical upset you are suffering now.**

5. **When you feel upset, practice a simple stress management technique to soothe your body's fight or flight response. Go for a walk, breathe deeply, and concentrate on something pleasant.**

6. **Give up expecting things from people who do not choose to give to you, be it a friendship, assistance with a project, or directions to their secret fishing hole.**

7. **Instead of mentally replaying your hurt, seek out positive ways to get what you want.**

8. A life well lived is your best revenge. Instead of focusing on your wounded feelings, thereby giving the person who caused you pain power over you, learn to look for the love, beauty, and kindness around you.

9. Amend your grievance story to focus on your heroic choice to forgive.

The Uncluttered Life

*"Remove the debris that clouds thought and vision and we
shall find the truth of our surroundings and ourselves."*
—Jane Tidbury, author of *Zen Style*

I am often teased about a round side table that once belonged
to my aunt. It's draped with a Victorian-era cloth of ivory silk, its
fine strands of fringe sweeping the floor. On it sits a small
wedding photo in a silver frame, diminutive glass sculptures, a
hand-painted porcelain vase, and an orchid, all gifts from dear
friends. To some, the table is a mishmash of clutter. To me, each
object is a treasure that connects me to those whose love is
represented there.

When we consciously choose what graces our environment, it
will harmonize with our inner journey. Our home will be welcoming, restful, and intensely personal. Rather than mimicking an
interior design magazine, each book on the shelf, every painting

on the wall, and even the decorations we use at Christmas will reflect who we are and what matters most.

As the need for more diminishes, appreciation for what we have increases. Our life bursts with abundance but not in the usual sense. We have more time. Rather than spend life's energy shopping for things we don't need, we can take long walks, read, or build a tree fort with the kids. With less to clean and mend, we can focus on pursuits that add dimension to our purpose in life and enrich our spiritual, social, physical, and mental experiences.

With an uncluttered life, we have more money. It's not that we earn more (although for some increased income is the result of uncluttering); we simply buy less. But when we do shop it is with forethought, not impulse, for we know that what we bring into our life must offer a purposeful or spiritual benefit.

An uncluttered life ends confusion. With things in their places, we save time and frustration. We ease through the day with confidence and clarity instead of spinning into a whirl as we run late, double-book engagements, or forget them altogether. With a schedule that respects our limits and interests, a written to-do list (not the one you carry in your mind), and joy in what we do, life will hum.

A life free from internal and external clutter is healthful. Research confirms that our physical environment, be it home or the office, influences how we feel internally. Organized surroundings positively influence our heart rhythms and blood pressure, reducing anxiety and tension. We smile more, breathe deeper, and notice the details around us. We can control many of the factors that shape our surroundings by reducing nuisance noise, eliminating visual clutter, and making technology our servant instead of our master. Taking charge of our time by under-scheduling leaves space for us to become fully engaged in what we do with reduced pressure and added pleasure.

The uncluttered mind allows space to nurture the childhood brilliance that creates entire towns from egg cartons and hours of)writer's problem with plot, or spawn a cook's ingenious fish sauce recipe. The uncluttered mind energizes us to think in new directions that can translate into serious money if that fish sauce is franchised or that novel wins the Pulitzer.

The uncluttered life unleashes joy. When we love what we do, when our work reflects passion and utilizes our gifts and talents, we excel and others benefit. Several years ago Bob and I took a city bus from La Jolla, a community at the north end of San Diego, to visit the zoo. The driver sang out the names of each stop and embraced each passenger with a unbridled smile and a neighborly hello. As the bus moseyed along, folks traded snippets of news. Although we were in a big city with big-city issues, the atmosphere on the bus felt like a small town church picnic—even though we were among strangers. While the driver provided transportation that respects the environment, he also colored his job with a joyfulness that bubbled like champagne.

The uncluttered life is filled with possibilities. I met Janet Stewart Lilly while biking a trail in Derbyshire, near the Welsh border. She had lived in London and worked for a national publishing firm. Now she operated the small tourism office where I had stopped for a map. She was refreshingly open and engaging, and before long she was telling me about the sweeping life change she and her husband, David, had made when they moved from the city. Janet explained why in a letter she later wrote to me:

I was quite happy climbing the corporate ladder. We worked hard, were paid well, and had plenty of disposable income for weekends away and holidays. Can you believe that living in a one-bedroom flat [in London] I even employed a cleaning lady! But the daily demands [at work] increased. Everything became impersonal and PC-based. I was up at 6 AM and didn't leave my desk until the mad dash home on the 7 PM train.

David had always wanted to restore an old property and so we started looking. I never thought I would be the proud owner of an expensive pile of stones, but here we are [in Derbyshire]. And what a life! I can't believe that I have become such a keen veggie gardener. I wear the same old clothes—what a relief from having to worry about your appearance. We eat homegrown food and I get lots of exercise in the fresh air. I also have time for others, time to write letters and talk on the phone, time for myself, time to cook proper meals. Even though we have given up some things—financial security, expensive clothes, and holidays—I wouldn't want to go back to the way we lived.

While not all of us wish to restore a derelict property or muck about in the garden, Janet's letter sparkled with the message of the uncluttered life—purposeful, creative, authentic, and mindful. When we release clutter, we harness clarity. Our goals are focused, our path is clear. We know what matters most and we discard the rest. We choose our experiences and don't let others direct our lives. Vicarious experiences are not for us. We want to taste and feel and be *in life*! We take the high road and recognize the right of all to live their own truth, even if it differs from ours. We put money in its place and know the difference between price and value.

The uncluttered life exudes peace of mind. Free from the weight of negative thoughts and toxic people, our life is filled with affirming and enriching relationships. In place of righteousness, resentments, grudge-holding, and jealousies, we find acceptance and compassion. When our world rocks and rolls, we hold on, knowing that life is textured with challenges. And when we take our last breaths, we'll know that the life we lived was truly ours.

KEEPING IN TOUCH

- Do you have a clutter story to share?

- Would your publication or organization newsletter benefit from an article about uncluttering life?

- Is your association or corporation seeking a motivating and inspiring keynote presentation or seminar leader?

Please contact Katherine Gibson through www.clutterbook.com.

R E S O U R C E S

The wisdom and thought-provoking information in a number of books, Web sites, and organizations guided me in writing this book. The resources cited in *Unclutter Your Life*, as well as related resources, are listed here and organized by chapter.

Chapter 1 Clutter: Trash or Treasures

Books

- ☐ Collins, Terah Kathryn. *Home Design with Feng Shui A–Z.* Carlsbad, CA: Hay House, 1999.

- ☐ Kingston, Karen. *Clear Your Clutter with Feng Shui.* New York: Broadway Books, 1999.

- ☐ Smallin, Donna. *Unclutter Your Home: 7 Simple Steps, 700 Tips & Ideas.* North Adams, MA: Storey Books, 1999.

- ☐ Tidbury, Jane. *Zen Style: Balance and Simplicity for Your Home.* New York: Universe Books, 1999.

- ☐ Young, Pam, and Peggy Jones. *Sidetracked Home Executives: From Pigpen to Paradise.* New York: Warner Books, 2003.

Organizations and Web sites

- ☐ **Professional Organizers Web Ring** (www.organizerswebring.com) is an international Web site with information on professional organizers in Australia, Brazil, the United Kingdom, the Netherlands, and North America.

- ☐ **Organize Your World** (www.organizeyourworld.com) is an international association of professionals with lists of organizers in Mexico, Central America, South America, Asia, the South Pacific regions, the Caribbean regions, Canada, and the United States. It has an extensive collection of articles, tips, and hints for organizing every part of your world.

- [ ] **The National Association of Professional Organizers** recommends accredited consultants.

  The National Association of Professional Organizers

  4700 W. Lake Ave.

  Glenview, IL 60025, U.S.A.

  Telephone: (847) 375-4746

  E-mail: hq@napo.net

  www.napo.net

- [ ] Visit www.organizersincanada.com for Canadian resources.

- [ ] **Professional organizer Christy Best** offers a newsletter and weekly tips on her Web site (www.clutterbug.net).

- [ ] **Professional organizer Karla Jones**'s Web site includes articles and advice (www.get-organized.com).

- [ ] **Messies Anonymous** (www.messies.com) and **Clutters Anonymous**'s (www.clutterersanonymous.net) Web sites offer information on support groups.

- [ ] **Smith College Clinical Psychology Research Labs**' Web site (http://sophia.smith.edu/~rfrost) includes articles and a bibliography on hoarding and obsessive-compulsive disorder.

Chapter 3 The Essential Traveler

Books

- [ ] Gardner, Alison. *Travel Unlimited: Uncommon Adventures for the Mature Traveler*. Emeryville, CA: Avalon Travel Publishing, 2002.

Web sites

- [ ] **The Compleat Carry-On Traveler**'s Web site (www.oratory.com/travel) contains several excellent pages with travel tips by Doug Dyment, including an essential packing list. The site's links offer useful and up-to-date details on all aspects of travel, including security bulletins, bargains, airport information, and destinations.

☐ **Rick Steves**'s Web site (www.ricksteves.com) is packed with travel information, including tips on packing light.

Chapter 5 Office Overload

Books

☐ Aslett, Don. *The Office Clutter Cure*. Pocatello, ID: Marsh Creek Press, 1994.

☐ Beardmore, Lori. *88 Feng Shui Tips and Ideas*. Nobleton, ON: Beautiful Leaf Publications, 2001.

☐ Wydra, Nancilee. *Feng Shui Goes to the Office*. Chicago: Contemporary Books, 2000.

Chapter 7 Inheritances: Who Gets Grandfather's Clock?

☐ Web site has **Who Gets Grandma's Pie Plate? Your Guide to Passing On Personal Belongings.** This program is produced by the University of Minnesota Extension Service. It provides people with practical information to assist in family decision-making when inheriting personal property. Products include a workbook, video, and an educator's package. Order from

University of Minnesota Extension Service Distribution Center

405 Coffey Hall

1420 Eckles Ave.

University of Minnesota

St. Paul, MN 55108-6068, U.S.A.

Telephone: (800) 876-8636

E-mail: order@extension.umn.edu

www.yellowpieplate.umn.edu

Chapter 8 The Time of Our Life

Books

- ☐ Cox, Connie, and Cris Evatt. *30 Days to a Simpler Life*. New York: Plume, 1998.

- ☐ Easwaran, Eknath. *Take Your Time: Finding Balance in a Hurried World*. New York: Hyperion, 1997.

- ☐ Quindlen, Anna. *A Short Guide to a Happy Life*. New York: Random House, 2000.

- ☐ Richardson, Cheryl. *Take Time for Your Life: A Complete Program for Getting Your Life into Balance & Honoring Your True Priorities*. New York: Broadway Books, 1999.

- ☐ St. James, Elaine. *Simplify Your Life: 100 Ways to Slow Down and Enjoy the Things that Really Matter*. New York: Hyperion, 1994.

Chapter 9 Tune Out the Noise

Books

- ☐ Berendt, Raymond, Edith L. R. Corliss, and Morris S. Ojalvo. *Quieting: A Practical Guide to Noise Control*. Honolulu: University of Hawaii Press, 2000.

- ☐ Berglund, Birgitta, Thomas Lindvall, and Dietrich H. Schwela. *Guidelines for Community Noise*. N.p.: World Health Organization, 1999. Also available online at www.who.ch.

- ☐ Fay, Thomas H., ed. *Noise and Health*. New York: The New York Academy of Medicine, 1991.

- ☐ Kawaler, Lucy. *Noise*. N.p.: John Day Publisher, 1974.

- ☐ Kryter, Karl. *The Effects of Noise on Man*. Washington, DC: Academic Press, 1970.

- ☐ Willits, Terry. *101 Quick Tips to Make Your Home Sound SenseSational*. Grand Rapids: Zondervan Publishing House, 1996.

Organizations

☐ **The Noise Pollution Clearinghouse** is a national nonprofit organization. Its Web site features extensive noise-related resources.

    The Noise Pollution Clearinghouse

    P.O. Box 1137

    Montpelier, VT 05601-1137, U.S.A.

    Telephone: (888) 200-8332 (toll free)

    www.nonoise.org

☐ **Right to Quiet Society for Soundscape Awareness & Protection Information** is an excellent site for education and advocacy. Its Web site links to resources worldwide.

    Right to Quiet Society

    #359-1985 Wallace St.

    Vancouver, BC

    Canada, V6R 4H4

    Telephone: (604) 222-0207

    E-mail: info@quiet.org

    www.quiet.org

☐ **The League for the Hard of Hearing** has an excellent educational Web site that includes information on National Noise Awareness Day and the effects of noise on children.

    The League for the Hard of Hearing

    50 Broadway

    6th floor

    New York, NY 10004, U.S.A.

    Telephone: (917) 305-7700 (Voice); (917) 305-7999 (TTY)

    Fax: (917) 305-7888

        or:

The League for the Hard of Hearing, *continued*

2800 W. Oakland Park Blvd., Suite 306

Oakland Park, FL 33311, U.S.A.

Telephone: (954) 731-7200 (Voice), (954) 731-7208 (TTY)

Fax: (954) 485-6336

www.lhh.org/noise

Chapter 10 Techno-clutter

Books

- ☐ Schement, Jorge Reina, and Terry Curtis. *Tendencies and Tensions of the Information Age.* Somerset, NJ: Transaction Publishers, 1997.

- ☐ Shenk, David. *Data Smog: Surviving the Information Glut.* San Francisco: HarperCollins, 1998.

- ☐ ———. *The End of Patience: Cautionary Notes on the Information Revolution.* Bloomington: Indiana University Press, 1999.

Chapter 11 Work: Tyranny or Transcendence?

Books

- ☐ Allan, James. *As a Man Thinketh.* Philadelphia: Running Press, 2001.

- ☐ Giardina, Ric. *Your Authentic Self: Be Yourself at Work.* Hillsboro, OR: Beyond Words Publishing, 2002.

- ☐ Halberstam, Joshua. *Work: Making a Living and Making a Life.* New York: Perigee Publishing, 2000.

- ☐ Helliwell, Tanis. *Take Your Soul to Work.* Avon, MA: Adams Media Corporation, 2000.

- ☐ Laqueur, Maria, and Donna Dickinson. *Breaking Out of 9 to 5: How to Redesign Your Job to Fit You.* Princeton, NJ: Peterson's Guides, 1994.

- ☐ Levine, Terri. *Work Yourself Happy.* Buckingham, PA: Lahaska Press, 2000.

☐ Sher, Barbara. *Live the Life You Love*. New York: Dell, 1996.

☐ Sinetar, Marsha. *Do What You Love, the Money Will Follow*. New York: Dell, 1987.

Chapter 12 TV: Prime-time Clutter

Books

☐ Anderson, Joan, and Robin Wilkins. *Getting Unplugged: Take Control of Your Family's Television, Video Game, and Computer Habits*. Hoboken, NJ: John Wiley and Sons, 1998.

☐ Bennett, Steve, and Ruth Bennett. *365 TV-Free Activities You Can Do With Your Child*. Avon, MA: Adams Media Corporation, 2002.

☐ Healy, Jane. *Endangered Minds: Why Children Don't Think and What We Can Do About It*. New York: Touchstone Books, 1999.

☐ McClendon,Marie. *Alternatives to TV Handbook*. N.p. Whole Human Beans Co., 2001.

☐ Postman, Neil. *The Disappearance of Childhood*. New York: Vintage Books, 1994.

Organizations

☐ The **TV-Turnoff Network** (www.tvturnoff.org) is an excellent site to learn about TV-free living and TV Turnoff Week, which is held each year in April.

Chapter 13 Cluttered Kids

Books

☐ Coloroso, Barbara. *Parenting With Wit and Wisdom*. Toronto: Viking, 1999.

☐ Elkind, David. *The Hurried Child*. New York: Addison-Wesley Publishing House, 1988.

☐ Hewlett, Sylvia Ann, and Cornel West. *The War Against Parents*. Boston: Houghton Mifflin, 1998.

☐ Saunders, Charmaine. *Teenagers and Stress*. New York: Harper Collins, 1998.

☐ Swigart, Jane. *The Myth of the Perfect Mother: Parenting Without Guilt*. New York: McGraw-Hill Contemporary Books, 1998.

☐ Witkin, Georgia. *Kidstress: What It Is, How It Feels, and How to Help*. New York: Penguin, 2000.

Web sites

☐ The **PTA** (www.pta.org) is the largest volunteer child advocacy organization in the United States. Information and discussion groups are available on its Web site.

☐ **Parent Soup** (www.parentsoup.com) is an excellent source for information on all issues of parenting, including child health, behavior, milestones, siblings, and raising teenagers. The Web site offers free newsletters.

☐ **National Network for Child Care** (www.nncc.org) is devoted to improving child-care and youth programs for infants and toddlers, preschoolers, school-age children and youth, and teens during out-of-school time, and offers excellent resources.

Chapter 14 Uncluttering the Holidays

Books

☐ Blahnik, Judith. *Checklist for a Perfect Christmas*. New York: Doubleday, 1996.

☐ Brucker, Virginia. *Gifts From the Heart*. Nanoose Bay, BC: We Believe Publications, 2000.

- [ ] Caplan, Mariana. *When Holidays Are Hell*. Prescott, AZ: Hohm Press, 1997.

- [ ] Hunt, Mary. *Debt-Proof Your Holiday: How to Save a Sleigh-Load of Money, Wrap Up Your Bills & Have the Happiest Holiday Ever*. New York: St. Martin's Press, 1997.

- [ ] Monn, David E. *365 Ways to Prepare for Christmas*. New York: Harper Collins, 1996.

- [ ] Rappaport, Herbert. *Holiday Blues: Rediscovering the Art of Celebration*. Philadelphia: Running Press Publishers, 2000.

- [ ] Robinson, Jo, and Jean C. Staeheli. *Unplug the Christmas Machine: A Complete Guide to Putting Love & Joy Back into the Season*, rev. ed. New York: Quill, 1991.

- [ ] St. James, Elaine. *Simplify Your Christmas: 100 Ways to Reduce the Stress & Recapture the Joy of the Holidays*. Kansas City, MO: Andrews McMeel Publishing, 1998.

Chapter 15 Friends: Soul Mates or Spirit-vampires?

Books

- [ ] Bradshaw, John. *Bradshaw On: The Family*. Hillsboro Beach, FL: Health Communications, Inc., 1989.

- [ ] Bramson, Robert M. *Coping with Difficult People*. New York: Dell, 1988.

- [ ] Gilliam, Joe, and Chuck Dyner. *How to Handle Difficult People*. Carol Stream, IL: Oasis Audio, 2000.

- [ ] Glass, Lillian. *Toxic People: 10 Ways of Dealing With People Who Make Your Life Miserable*. New York: St. Martin's Press, 1995.

- [ ] Weinhold, Barry K., and Janae B. Weinhold. *Breaking Free of the Co-Dependency Trap*. New York: Fine Communications, 1999.

Web sites

- [ ] **Mike Moore and Motivational Plus** (www.motivationalplus.com): Mike Moore is an international speaker who focuses on the role of humor, appreciation, and praise in human relations.

- [ ] **Words Can Heal** (www.wordscanheal.com) is a campaign devoted to eliminating verbal violence, curbing gossip, and promoting the healing power of words to enhance relationships at every level. Organization supporters include Tom Cruise, Goldie Hawn, and Robert Schuller. Articles and a free newsletter are available on the Web site.

Chapter 16 Guilt: Unloading Our Burden Basket

Books

- [ ] Borysenko, Joan. *Guilt Is the Teacher, Love Is the Lesson*. New York: Warner Books, 1991.

- [ ] Dryden, Windy. *Overcoming Guilt*. London: Sheldon Press, 1994.

- [ ] Tangney, June Price. *Shame and Guilt*. New York: Guilford Publications, 2002.

Chapter 17 No Doubt about Self-Doubt

Books

- [ ] Burns, David D. *Ten Days to Self-Esteem*. New York: Quill, 1999.

- [ ] Fisher, Robert. *The Knight in Rusty Armor*. North Hollywood, CA: Wilshire Book Co., 1987.

- [ ] McGraw, Phil C. *Self Matters: Creating Your Life From the Inside Out*. New York: Simon & Schuster, 2001.

- [ ] Nelson, Noelle C., and Jeannine Lemare Calaba. *The Power of Appreciation: The Key to a Vibrant Life*. Hillsboro, OR: Beyond Words Publishing, 2003.

☐ Wegscheider-Cruse, Sharon. *Learning to Love Yourself*. Hillsboro Beach, FL: Health Communications, Inc., 1987.

Chapter 18 Don't Worry. Be Happy.
Books

☐ Breton, Sue. *Why Worry?* Shaftesbury, England: Vega Books, 2002.

☐ Hallowell, Edward M. *Worry: Hope and Help for a Common Condition*. New York: Ballantine, 1997.

☐ Martorano, Joseph T., and John P. Kildahl. *Beyond Negative Thinking: Reclaiming Your Life Through Optimism*. New York: Avon, 1989.

☐ Metcalf, C. W., and Roma Felible. *Lighten Up: Survival Skills for People Under Pressure*. New York: Perseus Press, 1992.

☐ Potter, Beverly. *The Worrywart's Companion: Twenty-one Ways to Soothe Yourself and Worry Smart*. Berkeley, CA: Wildcat Canyon Press, 1997.

☐ Schaef, Anne Wilson. *Meditations for People Who (May) Worry Too Much*. New York: Ballantine, 1996.

☐ Vredevelt, Pamela W. *Letting Go of Worry and Anxiety*. Sisters, OR: Multnomah Publications, 2001.

Chapter 19 Money Matters: For What It's Worth
Books

☐ Benner, David G. *Money Madness and Financial Freedom*. Calgary, AB: Detselig Enterprises, 1996.

☐ Dominguez, Joe, and Vicki Robin. *Your Money or Your Life: Transforming Your Relationship with Money & Achieving Financial Independence*. New York: Viking, 1992.

☐ Merrill, A. Roger, and Rebecca R. Merrill. *Life Matters: Creating a Dynamic Balance of Work, Family, Time & Money*. New York: McGraw-Hill Trade, 2003.

☐ Needleman, Jacob. *Money and the Meaning of Life*. New York: Double-day, 1991.

☐ Rowe, Dorothy. *The Real Meaning of Money*. San Francisco: Harper Collins, 1997.

☐ Twist, Lynne. *The Soul of Money*: *Transforming Your Relationship with Money & Life*. New York: W. W. Norton & Co., 2003.

Chapter 20 Nudge That Grudge

Books

☐ Enright, Robert D. *Forgiveness Is a Choice*: *A Step by Step Process for Resolving Anger and Restoring Hope*. Washington, DC: American Psychological Association, 2002.

☐ Jampolsky, Gerald G. *Forgiveness*. Hillsboro, OR: Beyond Words Publishing, 1999.

☐ Kendall, R. T. *Total Forgiveness*. Lake Mary, FL: Charisma House, 2002.

☐ Luskin, Frederic. *Forgive for Good*. San Francisco: HarperCollins, 2002.

☐ Pennebaker, James W. *Opening Up*: *The Healing Power of Expressing Emotions*. New York: Guilford Publications, 1997.

OTHER BOOKS FROM

BEYOND WORDS PUBLISHING, INC.

The Power of Appreciation
The Key to a Vibrant Life
Authors: Noelle C. Nelson, Ph.D. and
Jeannine Lemare Calaba, Psy.D.
$14.95, softcover

Research confirms that when people feel appreciation, good things happen to their minds, hearts, and bodies. But appreciation is much more than a feel-good mantra. It is an actual force, an energy that can be harnessed and used to transform our daily life—relationships, work, health and aging, finances, crises, and more. *The Power of Appreciation* will open your eyes to the fabulous rewards of conscious, proactive appreciation. Based on a five-step approach to developing an appreciative mind-set, this handbook for living healthier and happier also includes tips for overcoming resistance and roadblocks, research supporting the positive effects of appreciation, and guidelines for creating an Appreciators Group.

Forgiveness
The Greatest Healer of All
Author: Gerald G. Jampolsky, M.D.
Foreword: Neale Donald Walsch
$12.95, softcover

Forgiveness: The Greatest Healer of All is written in simple, down-to-earth language. It explains why so many of us find it difficult to forgive and why holding on to grievances is really a decision to suffer. The book describes what causes us to be unforgiving and how our minds work to justify this. It goes on to point out the toxic side effects of being unforgiving and the havoc it can play on our bodies and on our lives. But above all, it leads us to the vast benefits of forgiving.

The author shares powerful stories that open our hearts to the miracles which can take place when we truly believe that no one needs to be excluded from our love. Sprinkled throughout the book are Forgiveness Reminders that may be used as daily affirmations supporting a new life free of past grievances.

The Art of Thank You
Crafting Notes of Gratitude
Author: Connie Leas
$14.95, hardcover

While reminding us that a little gratitude can go a long way, this book distills the how-tos of thank-yous. Part inspirational, part how-to, *The Art of Thank You* will rekindle the gratitude in all of us and inspire readers to pick up a pen and take the time to show thanks. It stresses the healing power that comes from both giving and receiving thanks and provides practical, concrete, and inspirational examples of when to write a thank-you note and what that note should include. With its appealing and approachable style, beautiful gift presentation, charming examples, and real-life anecdotes, *The Art of Thank You* has the power to galvanize readers' resolve to start writing their all-important thank-you notes.

Summit Strategies
Secrets to Mastering the Everest in Your Life
Author: Gary P. Scott
$13.95, softcover

Picture your hands raised in a victory pose. No one but you, enjoying your moment, your victory lap, your knockout, your achievement, your crowning glory—your EVEREST! From wherever you stand right now, *Summit Strategies* can help you reach your own personal summit. Through riveting accounts of lessons learned on the world's most perilous mountains, international mountain guide Gary Scott offers sure-footed wisdom that will guide you, step by step, until you are prepared to take on any life challenge.

Celebrating Time Alone
Stories of Splendid Solitude
Author: Lionel Fisher
$14.95, softcover

Celebrating Time Alone, with its profiles in solitude, shows us how to be magnificently alone through a celebration of our self:

the self that can get buried under mountains of information, appointments, and activities. Lionel Fisher interviewed men and women across the country who have achieved great emotional clarity by savoring their individuality and solitude. In a writing style that is at once eloquent and down to earth, the author interweaves their real-life stories with his own insights and experiences to offer counsel, inspiration, and affirmation on living well alone.

The Book of Intentions
Author: Dianne Martin
$16.95, hardcover

"I *intend.*" With those two words, our whole world can change. When we take notice of our intentions and take control of our intentions, we create a more harmonious and satisfying experience for ourselves and others. *The Book of Intentions* is a spiritual touchstone that will help you achieve your highest aspirations. In simple, resonant language, the book offers meaningful expressions of intention regarding all facets of existence, including family, friends, nature, society, and spirituality. Both powerful and practical, *The Book of Intentions* will help you take the first step in creating a more fulfilling life.

Believe to Achieve
See the Invisible, Do the Impossible
Author: Howard "H" White
$17.95, hardcover

Howard "H" White tells us: *Extraordinary people are simply ordinary people on fire with desire*—and he knows. As Nike, Inc.'s liaison for athletes such as Michael Jordan and Charles Barkley, "H" has had plenty of experience with superstars. But he didn't start there. He has known extraordinary people his whole life, from his family and friends to his coaches and teachers. All along the way Howard has met people who opened his eyes to his own abilities, and he's spent his life doing the same for others.

Full of behind-the-scenes moments with favorite athletes as well as funny anecdotes, *Believe to Achieve* is an exuberant collection of wisdom that will help you recognize the potential in yourself and see the path to success. It's a handbook for all people who have a goal they don't know how to reach or who want to help others discover their gifts.

Home Sweeter Home
Creating a Haven of Simplicity and Spirit
Author: Jann Mitchell
Foreword: Jack Canfield
$12.95, softcover

We search the world for spirituality and peace—only to discover that happiness and satisfaction are not found "out there" in the world but right here in our houses and in our hearts. Award-winning journalist and author Jann Mitchell offers creative insights and suggestions for making our home life more nurturing, spiritual, and rewarding for ourselves, our families, and our friends.

The Hidden Messages in Water
Author: Masaru Emoto
$16.95, softcover

Imagine if water could absorb feelings and emotions or be transformed by thoughts. Imagine if we could photograph the structure of water at the moment of freezing and from the image "read" a message about the water that is relevant to our own health and well-being on the planet. Imagine if we could show the direct consequences of destructive thoughts or, alternately, the thoughts of love and appreciation. *The Hidden Messages in Water* introduces readers to the revolutionary work of Japanese scientist Masaru Emoto, who discovered that molecules of water are affected by thoughts, words, and feelings. Dr. Emoto shares his realizations from his years of research and explains the profound implications on the healing of water, mankind, and earth.

To order or to request a catalog, contact

Beyond Words Publishing, Inc.
20827 N.W. Cornell Road, Suite 500
Hillsboro, OR 97124-9808
503-531-8700

You can also visit our Web site at *www.beyondword.com* or e-mail us at *info@beyondword.com*.

BEYOND WORDS PUBLISHING, INC.

OUR CORPORATE MISSION

Inspire to Integrity

OUR DECLARED VALUES

We give to all of life as life has given us.

We honor all relationships.

Trust and stewardship are integral to fulfilling dreams.

Collaboration is essential to create miracles.

Creativity and aesthetics nourish the soul.

Unlimited thinking is fundamental.

Living your passion is vital.

Joy and humor open our hearts to growth.

It is important to remind ourselves of love.